CALL CENTRE MANAGEMENT

A PRACTICAL GUIDE

by Janette Menday

©**1996** Menday, Janette
Call Centre Management, a practical guide
ISBN 0 9529239 0 4

published by
CALLcraft
The Croft Annexe
Ewood Lane Estate
Newdigate
Surrey RH5 5AP UK

CONTENTS

Introduction **5**
1 People **9**
1a recruitment 10
1b skill development 19
1c performance management 25
2 Service Levels **35**
2a call forecasting 38
2b agent scheduling 47
2c exchange lines 54
2d MIS reports 57
3 Technology **69**
3a ACDs 70
3b centrex services 79
3c diallers 81
3d computer telephony integration- cti 85
3e voice processing 90
3f workforce management .94
3g multi-media 95
3h scripting 99
4 Project Management **101**
4a siting 102
4b tenders 107
4c outsourcing 111
4d design 116
4e ACD configuration 124
5 Operations **134**
5a risk assessment 135
5b disaster recovery 139
5c health & safety 144
5d cost per call 148
5e teleworking 153
5f benchmarking 161
6 NORTEL **167**
6a The Nortel Meridian Call Centre - a background 167
6b Nortel in Europe, the Middle East, C.I.S. & Africa 172
7 Glossary **179**
8 Further information **187**
9 Index **189**

Acknowledgments

In researching for this book I thank Nortel, without whose sponsorship, interest and support it might never have got off the ground. All the information found in chapter 6 was supplied by Nortel.

I am indebted to industry experts at Aspen Consultancy who always patiently listen to my questions and even more patiently respond! Most of the information on risk assessment and disaster recovery found in chapters 5a and 5b and benchmarking in 5f was supplied by Aspen.

Thank you also to the following people who over the years have helped me gain a better understanding of the call centre industry, its technology and management;

Brad Cleveland, Jamie Clyde, Philip Cohen, George Cornelius, Rufus Grig, Dohn Kivett, Marcus Liberman, Paul MacAree, Peter Massey, Martin Meikle-Small, David Naylor, Clive Sawkins, Rob Smale, Phil Smith, Alan Vaughan, Marta Winks and Ken Wiseman.

Hearty thanks to two people who have shown exceptional tolerance in putting up with me whilst writing this book - my husband Paul and my colleague Frances Brookes.

Finally a big thank you to to my work colleagues Kirsty Hood, Lisa Lewin and Nicola Meehan.

Janette E Menday

Introduction

The power of the call centre

I started my career in call centres many years ago as a reservations sales agent for an airline. Around 25 of us sat in one long row with a couple of supervisors peering down at us from the top of the room. We had to put our hands up if we wanted a comfort break and then we were sometimes denied! We each handled between 150 and 200 calls per day from travel agencies and the general public, booking flights, checking fares and arranging tickets.

In those days telephone sales agents were regarded as 'girls on the phones' and the job was used simply as a stepping stone to reach other more important departments. My own ambition at that time was for promotion to work on an airport ticket desk. We were poorly paid and we were trained only in the product itself and how to operate the computer. The objective was to take as many calls as possible in the shortest possible time.

Very few people stayed in reservations longer than one year.

Each week a list of the top ten employees was pinned to the wall. To reach number 1 you had to handle the most calls in the week. The agent who was invariably the winner had an excellent method of doing this. After every three calls or so she simply put the phone down on the next caller before he had time to speak. Magic.

The phrase customer service had not yet been discovered.

In today's competitive world there is not a product that cannot be matched nor a price that cannot be beaten. Service is the differentiator, and service excellence is what the call centre can provide when managed well. As our customers become more sophisticated in their requirements, we need to ensure our service provision matches their expectations.

Customers expect their calls to be answered promptly. They expect their enquiries to be handled efficiently and courteously. They expect the information provided to them to be accurate.

To achieve this consistently, our call centres need to be managed effectively.

This book is intended for people who want a greater understanding of call centre management and of the role of the call centre manager.

Call centre management

Managing your staffing and service levels by matching agent shifts to call volumes, to achieve an acceptable balance of productivity and good customer service is the key to good call centre management.

So good call centre management is the art of having the right number of people available to answer calls and ensuring those calls are handled with high quality service.

This means forecasting calls accurately, understanding the peaks and troughs of call traffic and balancing this with appropriate agent scheduling. It means recruiting, training, coaching and inspiring people who are working in a very restrictive environment to offer high quality service at all times. It also means having a good understanding of the tools available to help and the barriers that exist.

However, there is no doubt that first and foremost, call centre management is about people.

It might have been logical to start this book with project management and conclude it with the most important element - managing people.

But, before you can commence a call centre development project, you need to understand the role of people within the call centre and the importance of service levels and the role of technology. You also need to learn the industry jargon.

With that in mind, and as the call centre is primarily about people, I have chosen to start with recruitment.

Your management style and the mix of people you employ will determine the culture of your call centre and will impact the entire operation. Recruitment, training and performance management are therefore the key drivers.

My fifteen years experience in the call centre industry has taught me that you can never hold all the answers. Each centre is different and has different needs and different service objectives. But there are basics that impact all call centres and it is these basics that I have chosen to address in this book.

Call centre management has developed its own professional identity and has become a highly regarded and specialist career. There's now a call centre study course available where students can achieve a coveted diploma in call centre management and there are special quality assessments that are available to call centre agents.

Nowadays the call centre has been recognised for its importance in both increasing customer service and customer retention and for revenue generation. It is no longer considered a cost centre but as a highly efficient profit centre. Call centre agents can now command a salary commensurate with their skills and their role of handling direct customer enquiries is regarded as key to a successful operation.

Instead of using the call centre as a stepping stone to other departments, many organisations now see the call centre as a career in its own right and work hard to ensure job enrichment and career fulfillment. Good salaries, good working conditions and good management are, thankfully, becoming the norm.

Welcome to all of you who are just entering the call centre profession for the first time, and congratulations on selecting such an exciting industry for your career.

CHAPTER 1: PEOPLE

A company is only as good as its employees and the key to any successful organisation is the people employed. This has particular relevance in the call centre, which is extremely people intensive.

Technology merely supports and facilitates the job of the call centre agent.

The agent

Each day each agent may speak with 100 customers and the way they interact will make or break the relationship between the customer and your company. Therefore agent selection and training is one of the most crucial elements of call centre management.

The supervisor

The job of the call centre supervisor can be stated simply - to ensure their team of agents are doing their jobs to the best of their ability. However, putting this into practice is highly skilled work. The importance of good supervision cannot be understated. It is the supervisors who will create an environment where motivation can flourish. They will encourage and praise excellence, they will coach and guide to help agents to develop their full potential.

The manager

Everything flows down from the top.

Your enthusiasm, energy and leadership will inspire your supervisors. Your fairness, common sense and ability to balance everybody's needs, will win loyalty from your employees.

1a: Recruitment

As stated, the importance of both good recruitment policies and procedures cannot be overstated.

It is essential to recruit the right people at all levels within the call centre. To do this, a recruitment method should be established that works within the culture of your organisation and takes into account the external environment, such as the local job market. Therefore the recruitment methods may vary but there are certain basic building blocks that need to be established and used.

Job Description

The first item needed is a job description, after which an employee profile can be created and appropriate interview questions developed. Finally psychometric testing might be used as an aid to selecting staff.

You may be fortunate in having a Human Resources Department to take care of all your hiring. However, this may bring you a different problem. One of the major barriers to good recruitment is the misconception of the role of the call centre agent. If your company is setting up its first call centre, it is possible that Personnel may not fully understand the qualities required.

This job is not simply answering the telephones nor is the call centre agent a glorified switchboard operator. The call centre is the hub of the company, the one stop shop at which all customers require the answers to all questions. Each agent is an ambassador of your company and may speak to over 100 customers every day, with the awesome responsibility of creating business or losing it.

It is a skilled job requiring a balance of exceptional qualitative skills such as communication, negotiation, empathy, patience, assertiveness and persuasiveness together with the quantitative skills of keyboard, computer systems and product knowledge. It is also a sedentary job, restrictive and excessively monitored. Although the agents work in teams, their job is solitary with little or no time to converse with team mates. However, they need to enjoy speaking over the telephone but must also control the conversation and skillfully close the call. In truth, finding good agents is an art which requires its own skill and an in depth understanding of the role.

In addition, the supervisory function is equally skilled, requiring a broad range of talents. The larger the call centre, the more specialised the role of supervisor will probably become.

The supervisor needs extraordinary people management skills to monitor, coach, guide and motivate their teams, and in small to medium call centres they may also need to call forecast, balance service levels, complete all systems administration of the telephone system and make dynamic changes as work loads demand. In 24 hour call centres it is not unusual for one supervisor to be completely responsible for the night shift.

The final job descriptions of both agents and supervisors will depend upon the nature of the work involved. Is it a help desk, a customer service unit dealing only with complaints, a sales office with revenue targets, or a debt collection service? Does it have extended hours and will the agents and the supervisors be completely multi-functional or will they specialise?

Once you have your job description completed, with a list of all the tasks you are expecting your agents to perform, you can then identify the specific skills that will be required to accomplish the job. After defining which of these you will provide training for, you will then be able to identify the skills you need to find in your applicants.

To complete this process you now need to create appropriate open ended questions. The objective here is to find those applicants whose responses clearly demonstrate that they fit your employee profile and have the aptitude for the job.

There would normally be four sections in a job description:

Job Purpose

A brief description of the role the individual would have and the objective of their employment.

Principal Job Functions

Here would be listed the principal activities that the employee would be expected to undertake.

Experience & Qualifications

Both of these items are divided into two sections - essential and desirable. As the words imply, the only essential experience and qualifications are those that are considered necessary to undertake the work and are not included in any training programme offered. All else is desirable.

Abilities

Identify which abilities are essential and which are desirable. Again, look at the competencies needed to do the job, and check which of these are included in your training programme.

EXAMPLE:

Customer Service section of a Tour Operator

JOB PURPOSE

To work within a team providing assistance to customers who have experienced difficulties with the product, and to resolve their problems, ensuring a high level of empathy and quality customer care is provided at all times.

PRINCIPAL JOB FUNCTIONS

- To work as part of the customer service team.
- To be available to answer calls from customers.
- To speak with customers on a variety of issues with a pleasant, confident, helpful telephone manner.
- To handle contentious calls effectively, with empathy and assertiveness where needed.
- To record details accurately into the computer system.
- To resolve difficulties by using the scripting responses or liasing with the floor supervisor.
- To calculate refunds based on scripting responses

EXPERIENCE & QUALIFICATIONS

- Previous experience of teamwork - essential
- Previous telephone experience - desirable

- Experience of handling irate people - essential
- Previous VDU experience - desirable
- Typewriting qualifications - essential
- qualifications in English and mathematics - desirable

ABILITIES

- Able to work as part of a team - essential
- Computer literate - essential
- Articulate speaking voice with excellent verbal communication skills - essential
- Demonstrate a calm manner and an ability to handle difficult people - essential
- Keyboard skills - essential

In the case above, you are looking for someone who works well in a team and is not required to use a great deal of initiative - most of the answers are in the computer system and the supervisor deals with the rest. They do not require foreign languages, however they need to enunciate clearly. Important skills are dealing with contentious calls and using the keyboard.

Once you have your job description completed, check the contents of your training course in order to identify which skills the prospective employee must bring to the job as they will not be provided by the company. Then look at the skill training you will provide. Decide whether the applicant needs to demonstrate an ability for this skill or whether training will give them the ability to perform satisfactorily.

You now have the basic outline of your profile and are ready to advertise the vacancy.

Recruitment Agencies

Many companies use a specialist recruitment agency, particularly if large numbers of agents are required on a regular basis.

Some agencies offer full time and part time staff for permanent secondment relieving you of the entire recruitment process and staff administration. This solution can also make it easier for you to increase and decrease your headcount when your work load dictates.

Using either approach, you need to ensure that the agency is fully aware of your needs and that the extent of the agency's involvement is defined. Perhaps you only want to use their services for advertising, paper screening or for assistance up to the first interview.

It may also be a good idea to introduce quality criteria into their contracts. For example you might have a 'pay only for successful candidates' policy, which puts pressure on the agency to find high calibre staff.

Whichever route you choose, your advertisement will need to state all those qualities and experiences that you feel are necessary. In addition those which are desirable should be stated as such. Make your advertisement give an impression of the style of the company - flamboyant and fun, established and reliable, etc. This will automatically attract the type of person who is more likely to "feel comfortable" within your culture.

Legislation in most countries dictates there should be no discrimination on the grounds of race, religion or sex.

However age discrimination, against the law in the United States still exists in Europe, and is even considered "acceptable". Many advertisements state 25-35 years age restriction. This results in many companies hiring only younger people and losing out on the experience and qualities of senior personnel. It is my view that a balanced office with a variety of age and experience, men and women, as well as a mix of cultures, creates better team work, maximises potential and enriches everyone.

A few things to look out for, in addition to the profile requirements, are job hopping which *may* be a trend showing immaturity or personality problems.

Paper Screening

You may be very selective in paper screening candidates, rejecting applicants based purely on their curriculum vitae (résumé). This does decrease the interview workload but too stringent a reduction at this stage may lead to rejection of potentially good agents. I do recommend that you use the telephone interview to play the major role in initial screening.

Telephone Interview

As we are in telebusiness and are looking for people who will be comfortable speaking on the telephone all day, our first interview needs to be over the telephone to determine the applicant's voice tones.

As the phone operator is usually the first contact for any new customer, the way they speak is of tremendous importance. Their listening skills and pacing to the caller are critical elements in customer service.

TELEPHONE INTERVIEW		
Voice tones and speaking voice: Candidate _____		
loud voice	*normal voice*	soft voice
speaks slowly	*paces with me*	speaks fast
monotone	*varied pitch*	excitable
impassive	*friendly*	curt, sharp
weak	*clear*	strong
uninterested	*enthusiastic*	agitated
poor grammar	*enunciates well*	unintelligible
mumbles	*articulates well*	harsh vernacular
uses slang	*eloquent*	uses jargon
digresses	*deliberates*	impulsively responds
requests you to repeat	*concentrates*	interrupts
misunderstands	*focused answers*	answers a different question

Therefore it is wise to use a check list that can be used during the telephone interview. This will help you determine the people with the type of voice that will project the right image for your company.

It may look something like the form on the previous page.

You may wish to keep this first interview fairly brief, no more than twenty minutes or so then short list candidates who would be invited to the office for the second interview face to face. Some companies do advocate scheduling up to a full hour for the telephone interview, and shortening the face to face quite drastically. This certainly gives you ample time to really test the applicant's telephone manner. Try asking questions speaking quickly to begin with and then after a few questions, slow down. See if the applicants change their pace to match yours.

Interview Questions

Our next stage is to devise our actual interview questions. It is essential that interview questions have been constructed with a full understanding of the process that is to be undertaken. Therefore if you are holding telephone interviews and subsequently face to face interviews, you need to think through what you are trying to test at each stage, reducing duplication except where you are testing for consistency of answers.

The telephone interviews would ideally consist of questions that will give a clear indication of whether this candidate fits your employee profile, and also ensures the candidate understands the role that they have applied for.

Face to Face Interviews

When you plan the face to face interview make sure that it follows on within a reasonably short time from the telephone interview, so that points raised are still relevant and fresh in your mind, as well as the candidates. You need to ensure that all the paperwork is ready and completed in a defined way and that you have read any information appertaining to the candidate. You need to decide beforehand which of the questions you are going to use based on your knowledge of the role and this particular candidate.

It is a good idea to give your candidates the opportunity to 'double jack', in other words to sit and listen in to one of your current agents.

This ensures that they gain a good understanding of the work involved and enables them to talk to someone actually doing the job. They get the opportunity to question the agent and gain a valuable insight into your company.

Undertaking a large number of interviews in a short space of time can be tiring and monotonous which can lead to mistakes and bad decisions. Break the day up as much as possible, without cramming in too many interviews yet maintaining the consistency you need.

For some roles you may wish to hold an assessment programme where you test skills and aptitude for team working, presentation and sales skills. Although this can be more time consuming and expensive in the short term, it can reap dividends in the longer term through higher quality of staff recruitment, less mistakes and lower turnover. If you do follow this path it is important to reduce your short list to a minimum through paper screening, testing and telephone interviews.

Make sure you feel confident with any decisions you make and don't feel forced into decisions for the wrong reasons, such as making up numbers or time restraints. An error at this point will cost both time and money later. For this reason it is essential to build the recruitment process as integral to the budgeting and planning process.

If you reject someone who is borderline, it may be worth giving written or verbal feedback to them and keeping them on your records. In this way, when either they have developed more competencies or overcome that particular objection, or if you are recruiting for a different role for which they are well suited, you have a short cut and a cheap method for hiring.

Once you have shortlisted your agents, psychometric tests can be utilised to confirm your assessments.

Psychometric tests

Psychometric testing can be used to support evidence from the interview assessment or can be used before interviewing starts as part of your screening process to reduce the number of candidates you wish to see. They also can be used to identify specific areas of concern to be probed at the face to face interview.

As such they can be a useful aid in the recruitment process and can provide an objective assessment of people at work, their abilities, potential and personal attributes. But be aware of their limitations, especially when used to self-justify decisions through trying to match your view of an individual against their profile.

Psychometric tests and questionnaires are widely used across all industry sectors - research suggests that 75% of large organisations now use ability tests and 55% use personality questionnaires - and there is general recognition that well designed tests can be a good predictor of job success.

Here the task is to find the best possible fit between people and the role they fulfill by matching the skills and attributes of applicants with a set of competencies which have been identified through careful analysis of the job for which they are applying.

Tests can be used to measure particular attributes, like being able to perform calculations, verbal and numerical reasoning skills, while personality questionnaires will identify people who will be a good 'fit' with the team or the organisation, those who will work well with clients and those who work best alone.

Reputable test publishers will require that training is undertaken by the people who are going to apply the psychometric test - usually at least a week's training in the use of ability tests and a further week for more complicated instruments such as personality questionnaires. This is intended to ensure that tests are applied under standard conditions, that appropriate tests are selected and scores are interpreted correctly.

There are a variety of psychometric tests specifically for the call centre industry available now from test publishers.

Once you have your teams of agents recruited, you now must train them.

1b: Skill development

It is essential in the changing economic environment in which we find ourselves that we are able to adapt as individuals, teams and call centres. To do this we must develop and evolve the skills of the people who work with us, as well as our own. You may well find several important issues difficult to manage if you don't develop your people potential:

- you may find yourself hindered when fast change or reactions are needed

- change will be difficult from within and therefore it will not be easy to make proactive improvements

- your people will have reduced morale which leads to increased staff turnover

Seems like these are three very good reasons to focus on people development.

Agent development

Identifying training needs is essential for the development of people. Their training needs will vary according to the different stages of learning and experience cycles.

The first stage of the learning cycle will be the induction training of new recruits, based on the gap between the competencies and skills you require and those that agents bring with them. This should be established through the recruitment methodology already described.

Induction training is likely to need classroom facilities for a period of time to learn essential skills and product knowledge, as well as an introduction to your expectations in terms of their performance and behaviour. In many jobs people can learn from their colleagues by watching and copying. However it is a little more complex to do this in the call centre, where all business is conducted over the telephone.

The job of the agent is made even more complex as they need to learn how to use the computer system in addition to their product knowledge, and to remember how to phrase words and offer good service over the telephone - all at the same time.

If your chosen ACD offers a telephone turret where two agents can plug both their headsets into the same call, sometimes called double jacking, then you have the ability to separate the two key elements. This is ideal for new agents.

Whilst the experienced agent is talking, the new agent can be keying in the information. Once the new agent is feeling comfortable with this, turn it around and have the experienced agent key in whilst the new agent talks.

One item to remember when scheduling your agents is that your call handling time may double when you have new agents taking calls, thus you may need twice as many people to handle the same number of calls.

Ongoing training and development is essential in order to support continuous improvement. Again, this training will vary according to the needs of the individual and it should be linked to the performance management system. This is where evaluation of performance is supported with specific training which focuses on the individual's particular weakness. This increases training effectiveness, reduces costs and targets relevant training, maintaining interest and motivation in that person.

Effective agent development helps create a culture of:

- continuous improvement
- agent empowerment
- personal accountability

Such a culture has many benefits.

Job satisfaction

Any organisation that develops such a learning culture where employees are encouraged to fully develop their expertise and knowledge and then utilise those skills, is enriching the jobs of the employees. Such multi-skilling enables agent empowerment, where the agent becomes the focal point of knowledge.

Job enrichment and agent empowerment result in job satisfaction and high level motivation.

Improved customer service

Where job satisfaction exists, there are high standards of customer service. The two go together and this is therefore the second major benefit. It was Richard Branson, entrepreneurial owner of the Virgin Group, that is credited with the saying 'agents are more important than customers'. My own maxim has always been 'happy staff make happy customers'.

There is no doubt, the greater customer service you offer, the more likely you are to retain your customers. The more custom you retain, the lower your costs as according to research by TARP Europe, the profit of a retained customer is the same value as the profit of five new customers.

Multi-skilling and pooling resources

Your third benefit is the pooling principle, which is discussed in the next chapter in some depth. In simple terms, multi-skilling means you are training your agents to become one large group, all answering all calls instead of several smaller groups of agents, each specialising in a different area.

The pooling principle basically states that the larger the group, the more efficient the call centre and the smaller the group the less efficient. If you multi-skill your whole operation, the chances are you will need fewer agents in total than if you have small specialist groups in order to obtain the same service level.

Although there is a cost to ongoing training, the benefits are extremely high and rewarding for everyone concerned. A call centre which believes in these principles can be recognised immediately by the energy and enthusiasm it radiates.

Agent empowerment

Let's just take a closer look at agent empowerment and personal accountability which tags on behind. To clarify one point. Agent empowerment does not mean agents are authorised to make whatever decisions they like, on whatever whim they fancy.

It does mean that you have parameters and strict guidelines in place which the agents use to make decisions. The agent will look at the criteria, check the information in the computer and will make a decision based on whatever it matches. The agent is then empowered to advise the customer of that decision.

You can sleep at night. Honestly.

This means that the majority of decisions, for example whether refunds should be granted, are dealt with by the agent and not escalated up to the supervisor. The agent job is once more enriched, the customer gets the one-stop service desired and the supervisor is freed up to concentrate on the more tactical and strategic demands on their time.

You would train your agents in how to interpret the guidelines and give them ongoing coaching.

Where you have agent empowerment, you will also have personal accountability. This gives employees a feeling of responsibility and involvement, which again creates high motivation and leads to customer satisfaction.

The idea of personal responsibility is that you are responsible for all that you do and whatever you do impacts the entire business.

Agent availability

Being available to take calls ranks as the one of the main items on the agent job description. If agents don't adhere to their schedules, are late back from breaks and lunches and take random sick leave frequently, that will adversely impact your entire operation. In the chapter on service levels, the importance of each individual agent is demonstrated and how just one agent can make all the difference. If you educate your agents so that they understand service levels and the factors involved in achieving these, you can make your agents accountable for their time and feel personal responsibility to the whole operation.

Include them in future strategy by asking for their ideas. If you have corporate goals, involve your agents in how they can help the company. For example, if your company's mission statement claims you will offer quality customer service at the highest level, what does that actually mean to the call centre? Your agents could be asked to quantify this and suggest ways in which they, as individuals and as a group, can help the company achieve this objective. Again, if each agent feels accountable, they are more likely to strive towards achieving those goals and feel committed to its success.

As with all training, agent commitment should be gained through the creation of a personal plan with a performance agreement made jointly between themselves and their supervisor. This plan also creates a blueprint for each individual detailing personal development and growth.

Supervisory development

The role of the supervisor is to manage teams of agents and the daily call flow. Therefore you are looking for individuals who have the potential to inspire and motivate people, developing their talents and increasing productivity. You are not looking for those who are the best at handling calls.

After promoting one of your agents to a supervisory position on a Friday, do you expect them to come in on Monday morning and manage their agents with skill and expertise? Or do you realise that no matter how much potential they have, they will still need that potential to be moulded into talent and that only comes through a mix of training and experience.

There are four key elements to supervisory training. First and foremost is people management.

People management

Your new supervisors will need to learn about monitoring and coaching techniques, unique to the call centre industry. They will need to learn how to evaluate their agents, and how to appraise them for improved productivity. They will need to understand how to lead, motivate and inspire their individuals to give their best.

Technical management

Like any new manager your new supervisors will need to learn and understand basic communication skills, presentations, time management and delegation.

Operational management

There are some excellent tutorials and seminars now available which get to the heart of managing a call centre.

Your supervisors will need to understand ACD technology and the information it places on the supervisor's monitor screen. They will need to know how to make dynamic changes when circumstances dictate, and what to do when something goes wrong.

Most importantly of all they will need to fully understand the ACD agent and team reports and learn how to use these to benchmark their agents, evaluate individual and team performance balancing this hard data with the quality of the agent's work and their overall productivity.

Ongoing training

The third aspect is ongoing training. Managers need to provide the supervisors with a forum for learning and personal development so that they can continually develop their skills. Create a training structure that will encompass all the skills needed to do the job well. You might consider a half day workshop for all supervisors every month on a particular topic, placing a team leader/lead agent in charge of the call centre.

One of the principles in call centre management is that virtually all of the resources made available to the call centre are designed to help the agents become more productive. Likewise, the supervisors must be totally focused on ensuring their agents are successful and productive.

Whilst you will be responsible for developing your supervisors, part of their supervisory responsibility will be identifying agent training needs and managing agent performance.

1c: Performance Management

Your managerial style will dictate the entire culture and atmosphere of the call centre. There is no 'right' way of managing, although there are many 'wrong' ways. You will find thousands of books which discuss motivation, delegation and time management. This chapter serves only to highlight the issues that have specific and major importance in the call centre.

Good management is balancing the needs of the people working in the call centre with those of the customers, and therefore the business. Successful performance management will take these elements into consideration. Effective communication methods are needed to ensure that everyone is aware and involved in all achievements and all future goals.

Communication

As the call centre is so people intensive and is the hub of the organisation often operating with extended hours, it is not always easy to achieve good communication. Poor communication is usually the biggest gripe in any call centre.

First there is the 'internal' communication, the information that needs to be circulated within the call centre itself, such as a new incentive programme or a change in rates. The regularity of this type of information will dictate how you accommodate it. If it is frequent, for example airlines that have daily schedule changes, price fluctuations, promotions, global taxes and passport details, you may need to have a ten minute team briefing every day, for every new shift. If changes are less frequent, perhaps once per week or per month will resolve this.

Complex information can be placed in bulletins in your computer system and agents given time to read these bulletins first thing every day.

Where wallboards (electronic display messaging) really do become useful (I am not a general proponent of them) is for important changes that occur during the day which can be displayed for everyone to see. Some companies are able to 'speak' to their employees through either the computer or via voice mail boxes.

Failing all technology, a simple whiteboard is effective.

Many managers operate a 'surgery' where they speak with representatives from the agent group - perhaps one from each team that has been *voted* in by the team itself. This enables you to learn about and deal with problems or complaints before they get out of hand.

More difficult to control is communication from other departments. The call centre must know what anyone else in the company is doing that may stimulate telephone calls into the centre. Whether this is an advertisement, direct mail or debt collecting.

Often the call centre is the last to know and yet is expected to handle sudden jumps in call volumes and deal effectively with customers who are more aware of a new product than you are.

Improving communications with other departments can be a lengthy process. It involves their education in the importance of the call centre, the impact on the customer and company when the process goes wrong and the great potential uses of telephony that they have probably not yet understood. Regular meetings with Marketing, Sales and Brands helps to reduce poor communication whilst multi-skilled project groups which include the call centre allow opportunities for you to highlight the importance of the telephone and demonstrate innovative ways it can be used for company benefit.

If communication is good, many of the demotivators that affect performance are minimised. Everyone is clear as to what is required, by when and everyone fully understands what happens when performance is inadequate.

Performance Related Pay & Incentives

The debate about whether or not money motivates rages on, but there is no debate about whether recognition of performance motivates. The question then becomes how does one recognise achievements - with money or alternative means?

I believe there is great merit in offering extra money in recognition of good work. Isn't that exactly what a rise in salary is usually about? But where a raise is permanent, irrespective of the standard of work achieved the following year, and its ability to motivate therefore short lived, performance related pay (PRP) is awarded only when certain goals are reached on an ongoing basis.

There are many companies not willing to take the risks associated with the introduction of PRP. There is no doubt it is fraught with danger. Too little reward will be ineffective and too much reward may jeopardise customer service. Getting the balance right is the key to a successful PRP system.

You need a mix of measurables to encourage an increase in both sales and level of customer service. Rewards simply for higher conversion may not be in anyone's best interests. Set ceiling limits to the number of calls, or the amount of revenue, to ensure the quality of service offered to non revenue generating calls does not suffer, and include quality as a factor in PRP.

Numbers are hard data, measurable and objective, but quality is much more difficult to measure and is reliant on the subjectivity of the supervisor. Each supervisor is different and has different standards.

This makes it imperative that an office standard in quality is defined and clearly understood. Different agent groups might be given different criteria. For example, in debt collection it is important to be courteous, empathetic and assertive and have good negotiating skills. For general enquiries, enthusiasm and friendliness might be more important.

If you are setting up a PRP system for the first time, involve your agents and listen to their views. The whole point of PRP is to focus the agents on the important issues, motivating them to do a better job. You therefore need their support if it's going to be effective. In addition to giving you their buy-in, they'll also offer you some good ideas and identify some potential problems.

To keep enthusiasm for PRP, the rewards need to be reasonably frequent - perhaps quarterly . This is a timescale the agents can look forward to and not lose sight of, and is more likely to keep interest high. As well as individual payments, also set team goals with the reward divided up between the whole team. By offering PRP for both individual and team effort, team spirit is encouraged and the weaker agents will be supported and guided by the stronger.

And don't forget your supervisors. If their teams make target, then let them enjoy a reward too.

So how much should companies offer? This will of course depend upon your budget, but it should not be too high to cause avarice and not too low to be insignificant. As a guide, 15 - 20% of an agent annual salary as PRP may be appropriate.

The whole idea of PRP is to increase levels of service and revenue and therefore the more you can do to help the agents improve their performance so that they achieve top rates of PRP will benefit everyone. Therefore your ongoing training should include the skills that you are seeking to reward in PRP, coaching your agents to improve their performance and increase their pay packet.

Alternative reward methods

For those who either do not have a budget or believe PRP is part of the 'motivate by greed and fear' syndrome, there are a variety of incentives that not only help motivation but add a little excitement and enjoyment to the job. These can also be run alongside PRP.

Having individual and team competitions running from time to time is a good way of keeping motivation high. The name of the game is to constantly think of ways to stimulate and excite, to ensure the agents look forward to coming to work everyday and to enjoying the social aspects of their job.

This might be as simple as arranging evenings out. These could be anything from meeting in a pub for a few drinks to getting the agents involved in sports teams competing with other companies.

One of the most effective ways to boost morale and maintain a buzz is to run productivity contests and games. Whatever you choose to do, ensure you offer both individual and team prizes to encourage personal achievement and maintain team spirit.

However, one of the drawbacks with individual contests is that your higher achievers will always win the prizes, and this will demotivate the rest of the staff, particularly the part-timers who won't ever be able to win. Everyone must have the opportunity to win on a level playing field. So, introduce a "best improver" category or give prizes to agents who increase productivity by a percentage over target. Ensure that the revised target is achievable, with a little extra effort.

Competition rules must be crystal clear and contingencies made for cheating (yes, there is always one that will). Anyone winning a prize that is not *deemed* as fair by the rest of the agents will cause more demotivation than you could ever envisage!

Offer spot prizes now and again for something different, like the first agent to sell 'five red widgets' receives a National Lottery ticket. Try putting them in balloons and hanging them from the ceiling for added effect.

No budget I hear you cry. Nothing in the pot for theatre tickets, meals out, catalogue vouchers or bottles of wine. Before you move on to the next chapter, there are ways of offering prizes that don't require a special budget. One of the most valuable and sought after rewards you can give is extra time off (fully paid of course). Naturally this only works well if you have seasonally low troughs, or your staffing levels are sometimes a little rich. I am sure there are many of you that don't have this option.

For those of you who are still sadly shaking your heads, there are two other budgets that might be hijacked to accommodate some interesting gifts.

First approach your sales and marketing department and see if they can offer you promotional items like company T-Shirts or pens, or even see their way to purchasing items for you as part of a sales drive. Involve them in your competition so they feel a part of it too.

If there are no other options available to you, use your stationery budget innovatively. This can be used to buy books, filo-faxes, diaries, pen and pencil sets and a whole host of goodies. The prizes don't need to be expensive.

Competition themes

To make a good competition you need preparation. And you need a theme.

Use a brainstorming session with your management team to create theme ideas. It is vital that all the supervisors are involved in choosing the theme and are all comfortable with the one selected. Without their support, the programme has little chance of success.

The best type of themes are those in keeping with the current objectives and ones which create an image of action such as "building", "attacking", "creating", "moving forward" etc.

Another item to consider when selecting a theme is the music you will need for your introductory presentation. Music is exceptionally important and will continue to trigger the memory of the presentation for many months afterwards. Your theme might be restricted to the music you are able to lay your hands on.

The timing of the announcement of the programme is also very important. One month in advance gives the employees enough time to look forward to it, and not enough time to get bored with it.

Designate the first day of the programme as a special day, introduce it with a humorous presentation by the management team. Encourage the agents to come in fancy dress, emulating the competition theme. Do take photographs all the way through and put these out on display.

Here are a few ideas for themes.

"Sailing into Sales".

- Every agent is a pirate.

- Each team has its own pirate ship.

- Objective is to reach various islands by winning sea miles and then the search is on for hidden treasure.

- Decorate the office with murals of exotic palms and silver beaches.

"To Boldly Go"

- In true Star Trek style, each agent is a space traveller.

- Each team has its own Star Ship.

- Objective is to visit various planets in the universe by winning space miles, and then finding precious elements.

- Go mad with suns and stars and meteors, perhaps there is an odd alien or two amongst the agents...

"Building the Customer Tower"

- Each agent is a builder.

- Each team represents a company, tasked with building a high rise office building.

- Objective is to build the tallest building with the most levels, each level bringing a reward.

- The office can be kitted out like a building site with scaffolding and hard hats.

In all these cases, agents win either sea miles or space miles or a floor for the building, by selling a percentage of goods or specific goods. Small prizes awarded to individuals give the incentive to keep going. However, the final winner is not an individual but the team that finds the most treasure, the most elements or builds the most floors and each member of the team would win a more substantial prize. So both individuals and teams are rewarded.

As such a programme may be quite lengthy and run for three months or so, I would not be tempted to run such competitions more than once a year to keep the excitement going and to prevent the agents from getting 'contest weary'.

In the meantime, surprise your agents with an ad hoc game just for the day, or for the week.

Making it Fun!

In the majority of companies, the agent is tied with a cable, not dissimilar to a dog's lead, to a computer for 7.5 hours per day, where you are not able to get up and walk around at will, where you are constantly monitored and everything you do short of breathing may be recorded and certainly ends up in a report.

You have to try and smile all day, and your voice must be as fresh at the end of shift as it was at the beginning. You have to be accurate, you have to be enthusiastic, you have to be nice to those who would not be nice to you.

And once someone has yelled and screamed at you, you have to put that to the back of your mind and answer your next call a couple of seconds later with empathy and friendliness.

It is a difficult job, a sedentary job and can be very restrictive.

The manager who can bring a little relief, a little fun and excitement into this type of work is a hero indeed.

There are several tried and tested ways of accomplishing this. For example, you can have Fun Days where you decorate the office with a theme and have everyone dress up, or Leisure Days where those who usually wear formal outfits may dress in jeans and T-shirts.

However, the key to success is to make these days *special.* If your budget allows, lay on a buffet for the agents. If you have no budget, see if all the employees, including you and your supervisors will bring food in to share with everyone. Make the *food* part of the theme. If that is a desert island, then select ham and pineapples, chicken salads with fruit and coconut. The more time you take to make this special, the more successful it will be.

Don't forget to use that all important background music.

Team Spirit

Always an important factor in any organisation, it becomes crucial in the call centre where all individuals need to work as one cohesive team if consistency of service is to be accomplished I would only add that it is important that your vision is shared by your supervisors and agents, that their goals are your goals and that they understand how these can be achieved.

Offering rewards and praise for individual achievement is important, but the group effort is equally so. Be wary of developing such competition between agents that the team spirit is devalued.

Discipline

In such a constrained operational environment, it is very important to keep discipline tight, but immutably fair.

I am always amazed at the innovation used by people to *not* do their job. Here are a few, some common and some inspired!

- Disappearing ten minutes before log-off time for a comfort break and arriving back just in time to log out.

- Breaking the connection on the headset cable so calls drop in, but go unanswered (be aware - this does not show up on ACD stats).

- Cutting off callers before speaking (this shows as a short call).
- Putting callers on hold in order to continue a conversation with another agent.
- Staying in wrap up after work is completed. Watch for this particularly at around five minutes to log off time.
- Arriving at work, logging in on time and then going to make a coffee.
- Coming back from lunch, logging in on time and then taking a comfort break or grabbing a snack.

The reason for belabouring this point is simply to bring a little realism into this book. You will find yourself managing some agents who, whatever you do, may never achieve an adequate performance. After you have exhausted all coaching and guiding techniques you may need to start disciplinary procedures.

How you manage these situations is not always up to you. I know several companies who will not back their managers when it comes down to firing an employee for inadequate performance. This means it is pointless to go through with any disciplinary procedures as you cannot carry it through. Check company policy with your personnel department and your superiors before you waste any energy on warnings etc.

If you find you do have to carry deadwood, it is important to keep the rest of your agents happy by ensuring they receive the praise and recognition for their good work.

Because of the nature of the job, and the number of people involved, being late is one of the 'crimes' that does need to be addressed. Lost calls at 9 a.m. either mean lost business, or the callers ring back later adversely impacting service levels and causing more lost calls.

It is not like office work which can be left for a quieter period in the day. Therefore each and every agent needs to understand the implications of not being on time for shifts, and the seriousness with which it is regarded.

And remember, lead by example!

Favouritism

The second biggest gripe in most call centres, next to poor communication, is favouritism shown by the supervisors or manager. This can result simply from the different management styles of the supervisors - John is soft and Janet is hard, to ad hoc decisions on shifts, holidays, pay rises, and to decisions on disciplinary issues.

There is no doubt that it can be difficult to deny a favour to a good agent who works hard and always volunteers for overtime and the unpopular jobs, and that it is equally hard to give a favour to an agent who expends more energy in getting out of work than if they had done the job in the first place!

Whatever decisions you make in your call centre it is critical to motivation that it is seen as fair by the majority of the agents. This does mean every decision you make should be looked at from the whole perspective. You need to be able to justify every decision. If you find yourself, or any of your supervisors accused of favouritism, this needs to be resolved immediately or bitter resentment will eat any efforts to motivate your staff.

Anticipate likely reactions to your decisions and try and work out in advance how to deal with any problems. You won't always be able to prevent them but at least you'll reduce them!

And if you do make a mistake and find you have upset or annoyed some of your agents by making a poor decision, eat humble pie and apologise profusely. Discuss with them what they feel you should do to rectify the situation.

CHAPTER 2: SERVICE LEVELS

The majority of call centres use the achievement of service levels as a mark of their success or failure. Service levels are the benchmark of customer service. They are also the key to determining the number of staff you require and the amount of exchange lines you need.

Service level is usually measured in terms of the percentage of calls you require to be answered in a set amount of time, e.g. 85% of calls within 10 seconds and this is written down as 85/10.

Caller tolerance

To arrive at your desired service level you need to ask yourself how long you can expect your customer to wait on the line until you answer? What do your customers expect? How badly do your customers need to talk with you, or do they move on to the next number in Yellow Pages after just a few seconds?

These factors, called caller tolerance, will influence the service level you will want to offer, and you may select different service levels for different call groups. For example, insurance companies may offer a high service level for sales enquiries, those most likely to call the competition if their calls are not answered speedily, and a lower level for claimants and those regarded as a captive audience.

You may even choose to offer different service levels depending upon the time of day. Business callers during the day may be less or more tolerant than home callers in the evening. There is no industry standard as service levels should be matched to caller tolerance which will vary on industry, service, times of day, week and season and the level of competition.

First however, let's start at the beginning and take a look at how a call is processed in simple terms, learning some call centre jargon as we go. *You will find a full glossary on page 179.*

Call arrives at ACD

The call arrives at the ACD - the Automatic Call Distributor (see next chapter), your telephone switch. The ACD is the heart of your call

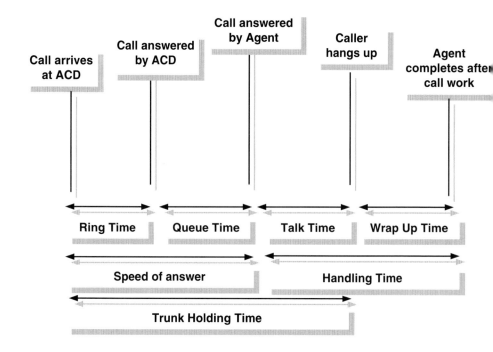

centre, pumping calls around the system.

If there is full *occupancy* with no agent sitting *ready* (or *idle*) to take the call, the call will ring out (*ring time*) until it reaches the time set by you for the delay announcement to cut in.

Call answered by ACD

At this point the ACD answers the call, offers some kind of recorded announcement followed usually by music. The call is then held in this queue (*queue time)* until an agent is free or the caller rings off (*abandons*).

Add the average queue time to the average ring time and you find the *ASA* - the average speed of answer. If the caller abandons whilst in queue (commonly referred to as a lost call), the time to abandonment is ring time plus queue time added together.

Call answered by Agent

An agent answers and *talk time* begins until the call is completed.

Caller hangs up

Any work related to this call that is carried on after hanging up is called *wrap up.* The *AHT*- average handling time of each call is made up of *ATT* - average talk time and average wrap up time which, just to complicate matters, is sometimes called after call work time.

Inbound calls arrive randomly and are the result of hundreds and thousands of people making a decision to make a call. However, although calls are random, there are general trends which enable prediction with some level of accuracy, called *call forecasting.* Call forecasting and AHT (average handling time) together are the two crucial elements in staff scheduling.

Erlang C

Call forecasting is accomplished by using a formula that takes random call arrival into account. The one most commonly in use is Erlang C.

Erlang C was developed in 1917 by A K Erlang, a Danish telephone company engineer. To this day, his formula is regarded as the most accurate method of call forecasting and is used in most call centres, and in software applications.

However, keep in mind that Erlang assumes random call arrival and that calls will queue when an agent is not available. This formula assumes that callers never abandon and never receive an engaged tone. This has resulted in some criticism that the formula leads to overstaffing.

As call centres have become more sophisticated and have established desired service levels, the call centre is now able to balance its staffing to minimise abandonments and busies whilst accepting that a percentage will hang up or will receive engaged tones.

So the first thing we need to do is forecast the total number of calls we expect to receive in any one month and then calculate the number we expect in any one day down to half hour slices. In a perfect world you would use 2 years of data to achieve a reasonably accurate result but if your call centre is new, you may have to use simple guesswork.

2a: Call Forecasting

You need to be fairly numerate to tackle this and if you have statistical experience, so much the better. We are going to look at some historical data and through various methods work out what the future call pattern might look like.

Calls usually vary by season, by day of the week and by the time of day. In addition, special events and public holidays will impact your figures.

When using historical data you need to decide whether you are going to use a simple average, use a moving average or a weighted average. A weighted average enables you to emphasise current trends and recent events.

In the following example, instead of adding the 5 pieces of data together and dividing the total by 5 to get an overall average, the information has been weighted so that the most recent information is given more emphasis.

EXAMPLE:

A SIMPLE SET OF WEIGHTS	
1.	07%
2.	10%
3.	18%
4.	25%
5.	40%

Calls offered on a Monday over the last five weeks.

1. 2378 (2378 x 07% = 166.46)*5 weeks ago*
2. 2327 (2327 x 10% = 232.70)*4 weeks ago*
3. 2298 (2298 x 18% =413.64)*3 weeks ago*
4. 1986 (1986 x 25% =496.50)*2 weeks ago*
5. 1928 (1928 x 40% =771.20) *Last week*

Total: 2,080.50

If you add all the figures together and simply divide by 5 you would forecast 2183 calls for next Monday.

However, by weighting each week's data as per the example above, you would forecast 2080 calls, 5% lower! If your business averages 100 calls per day per agent, this represents one full time employee.

There are three primary components of call forecasting:

- *TRENDS*

- *SEASONALITY*

- *RANDOM VARIATION*

Trends

In order to forecast calls we need to look at these three components separately.

month	call vol. 1994	call vol. 1995	annual trend
JAN	22,141	24,326	0.099
FEB	26,493	28,794	0.087
MAR	31,723	35,629	0.123
APR	31,984	34,828	0.089
MAY	30,867	34,268	0.110
JUN	31,879	36,333	0.140
JUL	29,147	33,211	0.139
AUG	29,421	32,198	0.094
SEP	25,741	28,937	0.124
OCT	24,978	27,439	0.099
NOV	21,410	23,214	0.084
DEC	15,120	16,329	0.080
add the trends together			1.268
divide by 12 to find the annual MEAN			0.106
divide by 12 again to find the monthly MEAN			0.009

Our first task is to calculate current annual trends, in order to quantify the percentage increase or decrease in calls. The formula to use is to subtract the older information from the most recent and then divide by the older as in this example:

(From JAN95) 24,326 - (From JAN94) 22,141 = 2,185/22141 = 0.099.

In this example, the trend for that period is therefore an increase of almost 10%.

Mean Annual Trend

Repeat this calculation for each month of the year. Add together the 12 individual annual trends and divide by 12 to give the *mean (average) annual trend* for that year. In this example it shows 0.106, or 10.6%.

Mean Monthly Trend

If you divide this mean annual trend again by the

months in the year (12) you obtain the *mean monthly trend*, i.e. the mean rate at which call volume has 'increased per month' over the last year. In this example it would calculate to 0.009, or 0.9%.

In summary, for numeral-phobes, this means that the current *call volume trend* is increasing by almost 11% annually or approximately 1% per month.

Seasonality

In order to determine true seasonality variations during the year, we must take into account the influence of the current call volume trend and incorporate it in our figures.

Stay with it!

No apologies here for those who are mathematically minded - you will find the actual mathematical formula at the end of this section. For the many people who are not, myself included, this is what you do.

Predict call Traffic

To predict your call traffic for next year, we start with the latest 12 months data. In our example it is simpler to start with December (as this is the most recent data you have available) and work backwards through the year to calculate *trend adjusted* figures (sometimes called detrending).

So, first take the last available month's data, in this case December (16,329). By definition there is no trend to add to the December figures. Therefore, the value of 16,329 is the one we must use for December.

November, being just one month behind December has to be multi-plied once by the mean monthly call volume trend plus 1. Therefore the trend adjusted November figure is 23,214 x (1 + 0.009) = 23,423.

For those who prefer to work in percentages, this is the same as multiplying the November figure by 100.9%, because the mean monthly trend is 0.9%.

October is a little more complicated, because it is two months re-moved from the latest data so we must take into account 2 lots of

month	1995 call vol.	trend adjusted figures (forecast JAN - NOV96)	*374,718/12 = 31,227.0 seasonality variation
DEC	16,329	16,329	16,329/31,227.0 = 0.52
NOV	23,214	23,214 x (1 + 0.009) = 23,423	23,423/31,227.0 = 0.75
OCT	27,439	27,439 x $(1 + 0.009)^2$ = 27,935	29,735/31,227.0 = 0.89
SEP	28,937	28,937 x $(1 + 0.009)^3$ = 29,725	29,725/31,227.0 = 0.95
AUG	32,198	32,198 x $(1 + 0.009)^4$ = 33,373	33,373/31,227.0 = 1.07
JUL	33,211	33,211 x $(1 + 0.009)^5$ = 34,733	34,733/31,227.0 = 1.11
JUN	36,333	36,333 x $(1 + 0.009)^6$ = 38,340	38,340/31,227.0 = 1.23
MAY	34,268	34,268 x $(1 + 0.009)^7$ = 36,486	36,486/31,227.0 = 1.17
APR	34,828	34,828 x $(1 + 0.009)^8$ = 37,416	37,416/31,227.0 = 1.20
MAR	35,629	35,629 x $(1 + 0.009)^9$ = 38,621	38,621/31,227.0 = 1.24
FEB	28,794	28,794 x $(1 + 0.009)^{10}$ = 31,492	31,493/31,227.0 = 1.01
JAN	24,326	24,326 x $(1 + 0.009)^{11}$ = 26,845	26,846/31,227.0 = 0.86
		374,718*	12.00

the mean monthly trend. Therefore the trend adjusted October figure is 27,439 x (1+ 0.009) x (1 + 0.009) = 27,935.

At first sight it probably seems a little confusing to multiply the monthly call volume by 1 plus the trend, then multiply it again by 1 plus the trend, (rather than 1 plus double the trend).

Don't give up yet!

The reason for this is simply that the figures need to be compounded much like earning *interest on your interest* in your bank account (or paying *interest on the interest* on your credit cards).

Correspondingly, September's figures are handled as follows.

$28,937 \times (1 + 0.009) \times (1 + 0.009) \times (1 + 0.009) = 29,725$

or 28,937 x (1 + 0.009)^3

The rest of the year from August back to January is treated in the same way.

You now have your forecast for the next 11 months.

We will need to use these figures to determine seasonality variations by comparing one month's figures, or a collections of months, to others. Then, in the event the trend changes, we can more accurately reforecast figures, by separating season from trend.

Calculate the mean monthly trend

First, calculate the mean monthly trend adjusted figure by summing all the individual monthly trend adjusted figures and dividing by 12.

In our example this would be $374,718/12 = 31,227.0$.

Seasonality Variation

Determine the ratio of each individual trend adjusted monthly figure to the mean monthly figure and you have the *seasonality variation.*

Hang on in there!

Using our example, in July this is 34,733 (the trend adjusted figure) divided by 31,227 (the mean monthly trend adjusted figure) = 1.11. 1.11 is the seasonality variation for that month.

Repeat this for each month. As a check on your mathematics, if you add all the seasonality variations of the year together they should always total 12!

Random Variation

Be aware of public holidays and other special events that may have impacted call volume on a particular day, or sequence of days last year, that may not be the case this year.

For example, in the West the Easter holidays are particularly awkward as they change substantially year to year, causing variations in the month of March and April whilst in the Middle East, Ramadan changes by one month every year and must be taken into account. You may also find call volume the week before and/or the week after a public holiday is different to normal weeks.

Watch out for higher call volume during marketing campaigns which needs to be adjusted but this is also excellent data to use when forecasting call volume for future campaigns.

Daily Patterns & Forecasting

Once you have your annual and monthly forecasts, you can now get down to the real detail of daily forecasts, instrumental in staff scheduling, granting holiday requests and managing the call centre generally.

Daily Index Factor

We need to find the call distribution pattern of each day throughout the month. In order to calculate your *daily index factor* (sometimes called day of week patterns) always find a few clear weeks without public holidays or other events which may have caused unusual call traffic behaviour.

Say you find six weeks of 'normal behaviour' call volume. First add up the six weeks and divide by 6 to get the *average weekly* total. (See table overleaf) .Calculate your *average daily totals* by first adding all your Mondays together and then dividing by 6, then do the same calculation for the 6 Tuesdays and the rest of the days. You can now calculate the daily index factor for each day by dividing the average daily total by the average weekly total. (Mathematical check - if your operation is 7 days, they should add up to 7!)

Half Hour Segment Index Factor

That wasn't too bad, was it? Just one more calculation to perform and you can start scheduling your agents! This is the *half-hour segment index factor.*

Half hour segments	Mon 1	Mon 2	Mon 3	Mon 4	Mon 5	Mon 6	Ttl	AVG %
0900 - 0930	17	23	19	26	22	18	125	**20.83**
0930 - 1000	28	24	33	29	31	22	167	**27.83**
1000 -1030	32	37	29	41	36	26	201	**33.50**
1030 - 1100	39	37	42	34	35	44	231	**38.50**
1100 - 1130	33	39	47	39	42	29	229	**38.17**
1130 - 1200	37	34	41	38	40	32	222	**37.00**
1200 - 1230	29	36	27	34	37	37	200	**33.33**
1230 - 1300	24	32	28	32	36	39	191	**31.83**
1300 - 1330	19	25	22	24	29	33	152	**25.33**
1330 - 1400	22	30	17	22	19	29	139	**23.17**
1400 - 1430	28	24	19	23	26	22	142	**23.67**
TOTALS	308	341	324	342	353	331	1999	

Use the same data from your six weeks of clear traffic and look at each half hour segment on the 6 Mondays. Add them together and divide by 6. Once you have performed this for all half hour segments during the day, you can calculate the half hourly patterns by dividing each half hour segment average for each day of the week by the average daily total for the same day of the week.

You made it!

These index factors are so important. Knowing the number of calls to expect in any one day is not enough. You need to know by each half hour how many calls are likely to arrive in order to schedule your agents appropriately. If you find your call volume increases over a lunchtime period, when you need to give your full time agents a lunch break, then you can resolve this by hiring part timers to fill that gap.

Public Holidays

Take as much historical data as you can to work out the index factors for public holidays. If you close on a particular public holiday which falls on the same day of the week each year, the daily index factor of each day of that week will be different to a 'normal' week, but its individual pattern every year will be be the same.

This enables you to make a good forecast for public holiday weeks. You may find the days of the week before each public holiday have different index factors and the call volume for that week may also show a proportionate lower or higher figure to 'normal' weeks.

Mathematical Formula

For those who are numeral-philes, I promised a mathematical formula. This formula enables you to forecast a specific half hour period next year.

Where:

a = Current Year's calls

b = Mean monthly trend adjustment

c = Forecast for year ($c = a \times b$)

d = Monthly seasonality variation

e = Forecast for the month ($e = c \times d$)

f = No. of operational days in month

g = Average calls per day $\left(g = \dfrac{e}{f} \right)$

h = Daily index factor

k = Forecast for the day ($k = g \times h$)

m = Half-hour segment index factor

n = Forecast for the half-hour segment ($n = k \times m$)

Then:
$$\left(\frac{(a \times b) \times d}{f} \right) \times h \times m = n$$

Or for the numeral-phobes:

Say we want to forecast a half hour period on a Monday in March next year.

We take the current year's calls (a), multiply by the mean monthly trend (b) to get the annual forecast (c).

Then multiply this answer (c) by the seasonality variation of the appropriate month (March) (d).

Take this sum, which is your forecast for the month (e) and divide by the number of operational days in that month (f) to give you the average calls per day (g).

Then multiply this by the appropriate daily index factor (Monday) (h) and this gives you the forecast for that specific day (k).

Now adjust this by multiplying by the half-hour segment index factor (m) and hey presto, you have your forecast (n).

Mornings often set the tone for the day. If by 10 a.m. you find more calls offered than you would expect, you can use the call volume for that hour to revise your forecast for the day.

Take the 2 half-hour segments, and divide by the appropriate half-hour segment index factors. This gives you the revised forecast for the whole day. Now multiply by the half-hour segment index factors to give you revised forecasts for each half hour period for the remainder of the day. This gives you the opportunity to make changes in order to cope with the extra workload and maintain service levels.

Now that we know how many calls to expect next year, we are ready to calculate the number of staff we need.

2b: Agent Scheduling

The number of staff you need is absolutely dependent upon the average handling time of your calls, the number of calls you expect to receive and the service level you wish to achieve.

However, it is not enough to simply multiply the calls forecasted by the average handling time because calls arrive randomly. If your forecast tells you to expect 200 calls each half-hour segment, you will find fluctuations where you receive 220 calls one segment and 180 another. However, by using Erlang calculations, you can work out the number of staff you will need to achieve your desired service levels.

Erlang Calculators

I toyed with the idea of explaining Erlang in depth, and even printing the tables so that you could work out your own calculations. However, there are now so many Erlang calculators on the market that I decided it would be as silly as offering you multiplication tables.

The friendliest calculator I have used is from the Incoming Calls Management Institute (ICMI) in the USA. However, one that has been freely available is supplied by workforce management specialists, TCS - contact your local office. Alternatively take a look at the call centre internet pages - http://www.callcentre.co.uk and check out what is available at the moment. A British firm, Quality Plus Consulting are currently offering a free calculator.

With most of the calculators, all you have to do is input your call forecast per half hour, the average talk time and wrap up time (AHT) and your desired service level. The calculators then work out the number of agents needed to achieve that service level.

You may use a typical desired service level, for example, of answering 90% of all inbound calls within 20 seconds, or may be one more stringent, say 95% of calls in 5 seconds. As mentioned earlier, your desired service level will usually reflect your callers' tolerance. In addition you may also have parameters for abandoned calls - perhaps no more than 5% is acceptable.

Naturally enough if you add staff, your service level improves. But there comes a point when the law in diminishing returns means it becomes unproductive to do this.

Adding staff has less of an impact on service level than subtracting them.

This is a fundamental issue for all call centre managers.

In this figure you can see that with 36 agents the service level could not be much worse with only 5% of calls answered within the required number of sec-

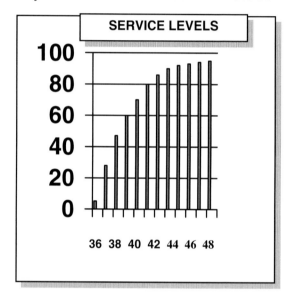

onds. You only need to add one more agent and the service level improves to 28%, add a second agent and you jump up to nearly 50%.

From the starting point of 36 agents, to reach the desired 80% service level you need only 5 more. However, if you add still another 5 agents, the returns diminish substantially. The difference between 43 agents and 47 agents is only an extra 4% of calls answered in the required time. With 41 agents, add 2 agents and your service level improves by 10%, but deduct two agents and it falls by 20%.

At this point it makes no sense to add any more staff. Each individual becomes less and less productive as their idle time - the time spent ready and waiting for a call - increases. On the other hand, if your service levels are very poor, you can make drastic improvements simply by adding one more agent. One agent can make a huge difference.

If you are forecasting poor service levels due to extraordinary circumstances, then even if it is just for your agents (and not senior management) reduce your desired service level goals for that period. There is nothing more demotivating for your agents than to know they cannot achieve targets.

So let's move on to productivity and occupancy. This is the amount of time an agent is occupied either in talk time or wrap up. The remainder of their time at work is unproductive, either waiting for a call to come in, or unavailable to take a call.

This takes us to the fundamental relationship between service levels and occupancy. If your agents are occupied 100% of the day, that means there will always be a call waiting.

100% occupancy results in poor service levels.

Brad Cleveland, one of the American gurus of call centre service levels, states that studies suggest occupancy becomes too high when it reaches 92% for an extended period of time (say several half hours in a row).

Also, the impact of taking one call after another, without any pause for breath, becomes very distressing for the agents. If such a situation becomes the norm, you will find absenteeism rises sharply. This creates a vicious circle where service levels then drop and occupancy goes higher still.

100% occupancy is bad for business.

This is a principle that your senior management need to understand, if you are to achieve good service levels with an appropriate number of staff, and not become a sweat shop offering poor service to your customers.

Occupancy percentages can be misleading. A call centre may be struggling to reach an 85% service level yet only have 65% occupancy. Random call arrival means that the time agents are ready, waiting for an incoming call, is split into small slivers of a few seconds here, and a few seconds there which can add up to a not insignificant amount of time.

Conversely, low occupancy where agents spend more time waiting for calls to come in can be equally bad. The less you do, the less you want to do and agents soon become bored and demotivated. It also means your business is paying for more employees than you require, and people are the most expensive resource you have.

The size of your call centre will also impact individual productivity as we are dealing with random call arrival.

Think of a single carriageway and a four lane highway where in both cases you want to achieve steady movement of vehicles. You only need one slow truck for the single carriageway to have cars 'bunching up' creating slow moving traffic and possible jams. On the four lane highway, vehicles have the option of three more lanes. All in all, the four lane highway can take substantially more than 4 times the vehicles than the single carriageway, with no delay to the traffic.

The pooling principle

The larger the call centre, each agent handles more calls to achieve the same service level, thus the more productive each agent becomes. In small call centres, you need more agents to achieve the same standards and thus each agent has higher ready time and lower occupancy.

Let's look at an example. See the table, if you take an average talk time of 180 seconds, and average wrap up of 30 seconds you have an average handling time of 210 seconds. Using an example with a forecast of 100 calls each half hour, in order to achieve a service level of 80% of all calls answered within 20 seconds you need 15 agents. The average speed of answer is 17 seconds per call.

14 agents will achieve a service level of only 67% and 16 agents will achieve 89%.

15 agents handle 100 calls			
Agents	ASA	S/L	OCC
12	561	14%	97%
13	97	46%	90%
14	37	67%	83%
15	17	80%	78%
16	8	89%	73%
17	4	94%	69%
18	2	97%	65%
19	1	98%	61%
20	0	99%	58%

Source: Incoming Calls Management Institute

However if you increase your calls tenfold to 1,000 you find you do not require ten times the number of agents to reach the same service level.

In this following example you only need 124 agents to achieve 80% and you also find the average speed of answer is much improved at 11 seconds. 123 agents will give you 75% and 125 agents, 85%.

Take a look at the occupancy figures, and see how much more productive each agent is in the larger call centre to achieve the same service level.

The larger centre can afford to increase its service level goal to 91%, employing just 3 more agents to avoid agent burn out. Occupancy of 94% is just a little too high and may cause stress, increasing the absenteeism rates.

124 agents handle 1,000 calls			
Agents	ASA	S/L	OCC
121	29	61%	96%
122	20	69%	96%
123	15	75%	95%
124	**11**	**80%**	**94%**
125	9	85%	93%
126	7	88%	93%
127	5	91%	92%
128	4	93%	91%
129	3	94%	90%

Source: Incoming Calls Management Institute

As you can see, the pooling principle can bring great productivity rewards. ACDs can now be networked across continents, enabling multiple call centres and single agents working from home to become part of one large virtual call centre. You no longer need to house all your agents under one roof.

Shrinkage

So let's figure out how many agents we need to schedule. Although we have calculated how many agents we require to handle our calls, we need to take into account absenteeism, lunches, breaks, training and any other situation that results in agent unavailability.

These numbers are of vital importance to every call centre manager and are called *shrinkage.* Shrinkage usually works out at 15% - 50% dependent upon your training schedules and holiday allowances.

To work out your shrinkage rates you need to calculate the percentage of time spent, in any one week, on absenteeism as an average per agent. This example shows a 40 hour week, 260 day year (based on Monday-Friday) with an agent shrinkage of 29.04%.

If your Erlang calculation lets you know that 25 full time agents are required on any one day, multiply this figure by the agent shrinkage to find the number of FTE (full time equivalent) agents you will need to hire. In this example you would multiply 25 by 29.04% and would hire an FTE of 32.26 agents.

Reasons for Absenteeism	Time	Percentage avg of 40 hour week
Paid breaks	2 x 15 mins daily	6.25%
Sickness	5 days per annum	1.92%
Training	10 days per annum	3.85%
Holidays	20 days per annum	7.69%
Public Holidays	8 days per annum	3.08%
Meetings, Briefings	1.25 hours per week	3.12%
Miscellaneous	15 mins per day	3.13%
Total Agent Shrinkage		**29.04%**

Agent Index factors

For day to day staff scheduling, you need to work out your *agent index factors*, sometimes called *rostered staff factors*. You have your calculation of number of agents required per half hour segments to be plugged in and on the phones (as per the erlang calculations). Now you need to figure in your lunches, breaks and any training for that day plus all briefings or meetings. *See the table overleaf.*

This gives you the agent index factor.

You need to know your desired service level, the maximum number of calls you anticipate at peak times and average handling times (talk time plus wrap up). This is sometimes referred to as the *calling load.*

Adherence Factor

Random call arrival cannot be controlled. Both service levels and occupancy can be manipulated through good call forecasting and staff planning. However, agent *availability* can be controlled, and this is called the '*adherence factor*'. This is the measure of how closely agents adhere to their schedules, being available to take calls when your forecast dictates you need them.

Agent Index Factor example

Half hour segments	agts per erlang	Break (15mins each)		Lunch 1 hour	no. agts needed	agt index factor
0730 - 0800	2				2	2/2 = 1.000
0800 - 0830	3				3	3/3 = 1.000
0830 - 0900	4				4	4/4 = 1.000
0900 - 0930	12				12	12/12 = 1.000
0930 - 1000	14	2	2		16	16/14 = 1.143
1000 - 1030	15	2	2		17	17/15 = 1.133
1030 - 1100	15	2	1		17	17/15 = 1.133
1100 - 1130	16	1	1		17	17/16 = 1.062
1130 - 1200	15	2	2		17	17/15 = 1.133
1200 - 1230	13			4	17	17/13 = 1.308
1230 - 1300	13			4	17	17/13 = 1.308
1300 - 1330	9			9	18	18/9 = 2.000
1330 - 1400	9			9	18	18/9 = 2.000
1400 - 1430	14			4	18	18/14 = 1.286
1430 - 1500	15			4	19	19/15 = 1.267
1500 - 1530	16	3	3		19	19/16 = 1.187
1530 - 1600	17	2	2		19	19/17 = 1.118
1600 - 1630	18	1	1		19	19/18 = 1.056
1630 - 1700	16	3	3		19	19/16 = 1.187
1700 - 1730	12	1			13	13/12 = 1.083
1730 - 1800	3				3	3/3 = 1.000
1800 - 1830	2				2	2/2 = 1.000

2c Exchange Lines

The number of exchange lines you need is directly related to your service levels. Remember the single carriageway and the four lane motorway. Whilst you have a traffic jam on your single carriageway, no more cars can get on to the road. It's completely blocked. If you add more lanes, cars can then move more freely, the traffic jam disappears and everyone can get on to the highway.

Likewise, if you have calls backed up and waiting in queue, using up all the exchange lines, other callers are receiving an engaged tone and you are losing business. However, if you add agents to improve your service level, calls are answered more quickly, freeing up the exchange lines to receive more calls. In these circumstances, the fix is not to increase your exchange lines, but to increase your staffing.

You need to be aware of average trunk holding times, the time from a caller completing dialling to the time the caller hangs up. During this period, one of your exchange lines is being used. There comes a point of course when you have plenty of staff, but the sheer volume of calls results in *ATB* - all trunks busy and calls cannot get through to your 'ready' agents.

Line Utilisation Reports

Most ACDs offer a trunk report, usually called *Line Utilisation* which demonstrates any ATB periods. The higher the percentage of ATB, the more likely some of your customers are receiving an engaged (busy) tone when they call you.

Once you have forecasted the number of anticipated calls, calculated the call handling time and the number of staff you need, you can then work out the number of exchange lines necessary to carry the traffic. As we now understand, high occupancy and low service levels cause delay to call flow, therefore you cannot calculate the number of exchange lines you need before you have calculated the number of staff required.

Now there are two approaches to calculating the number of lines you need.

The first approach is to calculate the call volume, multiply by the average talk time plus the average speed of answer and convert this into hours. Then look this up in Erlang B tables (every good communications manager will have these!)

Centum Calling Seconds (CCS)

Hours of workload are sometimes called erlangs. This expression is most commonly used when assessing trunk requirements, which are expressed in hours of traffic. This is usually calculated in blocks of 100 seconds, called *CCS* - centum (100) calling seconds.

Therefore one erlang (1 hour) is 36 CCS of call traffic (36 x 100 = 3600 seconds/60 = 60 minutes/60 = 1hour)

To calculate the call load, take the call volume over 1 hour and multiply this by the sum of ring time, queue time and talk time which is called the average trunk hold time.

For example, 200 calls with average trunk holding time of 4 mins would equate to 800 minutes or 48,000 seconds. This, when divided by 100 gives you 480 CCS. As one erlang is 36 CCS, you need to divide 480 by 36 which calculates to 13.33 erlangs.

You therefore need 14 exchange lines to accommodate this number of calls.

Or you could have simply taken the 200 calls, multiply by the average trunk holding time of 4 minutes to get 800 minutes and then divide by 60 to find the number of erlangs (hours). But then you wouldn't know about CCS and this is what often shows on your ACD reports!

Alternatively, simply stop adding exchange lines when the ASA is about the same as the average time to abandonment. At this point, any more exchange lines can only result in poorer service levels as more calls are able to get through. Where you have too many exchange lines for the number of agents available to answer them, you can, as a stop gap, busy out lines, sending an engaged signal to callers, rather than have them holding and abandoning. However, this procedure, called back busy, does distort all your call forecasting so it is not recommended except as an emergency measure in a difficult situation.

Back Busy

If you have taken over a call centre and find your call volume immediately increases and your service level drops through the floor, check and see if your predecessor has used this back busy function to prevent calls getting through in order to be seen as achieving service level. Naughty.

2d: MIS Reports

Your ACD will offer you standard reports with which to measure and manage your call centre, both dynamic (often referred to as real time) and historic. Many now offer a degree of customisation, enabling you to design your own reports in whatever style you like. Some systems allow you to import the data into Excel or other software packages, giving you great flexibility.

Historical Reports

Standard reports can be divided into Agent Data, Call Data and Trunk Data. As they imply, Agent Data looks at what the agents are doing as individuals, teams and as an overall office average while Call Data tracks inbound and outbound calls, identifying where they route to and when and where they are handled or lost. The Trunk Data looks at how busy the lines are and exposes line problems.

Reports can be pulled in a variety of ways.

Interval reports

Detailed interval reports can be scheduled which normally show activity in half hour segments throughout the day, or these can be requested on an ad hoc basis for any specific half hour segment or segments.

They are useful for evaluating overall call forecasting, workforce management planning and adherence to schedules. They also pinpoint success and failure with your service level achievement. You may have made your target for the day, but when broken down into half hour segments you could find that for half the day you were overstaffed and the remainder understaffed with your level of service seesawing throughout the day.

Daily reports

These normally show the totals for the whole day and offer more of a 'large picture' view of the day's activity. Exceptionally useful are the abandoned call report, individual agent performance report and of course the day's overall service level achievement.

Each ACD offers the information in a different way, with completely different codes and jargon, but the basic information should be the same, whichever switch you select.

Agent Data

Unfortunately there are no actual industry standards for jargon used on these reports and it can be quite a task to figure out what they mean. Your ACD manual should clarify each topic, but I have found many instances where their explanation falls short.

Looking at the example shown below, taken from the Meridian MAX Supervisor's User Guide, you have the following information:

Intervals

The time frame requested for this specific report.

Agt ID

The personal number given to each agent which they use to log in to the ACD, enabling the ACD to identify and track them.

Agent by ACD-DN Performance Interval Report

courtesy of Nortel showing Meridian MAX standard management report

```
                       Agent by ACD-DN Performance              Page 1
                           Interval Report

ABC Corporation                        Date: 04/20/95    Time:20:05:53

Intervals: 08:00-09:00      Day:04/20/95
AGT    INTVL ACD-DN  --ACD CALLS--     --NON ACD CALLS--    TOTAL  TIME-  ACD/
ID                   NUM  AVG   AVG   NUM  NUM  TIME  TIME   NOT    LOGN   LOGN
                     ANSWD TALK  WAIT  IN   OUT  IN    OUT    RDY           %
                          SEC   SEC              HH:MM HH:MM  HH:MM  HH:MM
```

AGT ID	INTVL	ACD-DN	NUM ANSWD	AVG TALK SEC	AVG WAIT SEC	NUM IN	NUM OUT	TIME IN HH:MM	TIME OUT HH:MM	TOTAL NOT RDY HH:MM	TIME- LOGN HH:MM	ACD/ LOGN %
1011	08:30	6100	10	128	25	0	0	0:00	0:00	0:04	0:30	86
	09:00		11	117	12	0	0	0:00	0:00	0:06	0:30	93
1011			21	122	18	0	0	0:00	0:00	0:10	1:00	89
1034	08:30	6100	11	71	29	0	0	0:00	0:00	0:01	0:20	73
	09:00		14	99	8	0	0	0:00	0:00	0:05	0:30	94
1034			25	85	18	0	0	0:00	0:00	0:06	0:50	83
1036	08:30	6100	13	102	16	0	0	0:00	0:00	0:04	0:30	89
	09:00		0	0	0	0	0	0:00	0:00	0:30	0:30	100
1036			13	51	8	0	0	0:00	0:00	0:34	1:00	94
1038	08:30	6100	5	207	10	0	0	0:00	0:00	0:02	0:20	96
	09:00	5900	10	110	10	0	1	0:00	0:02	0:02	0:24	84
1038			15	158	10	0	1	0:00	0:02	0:04	0:45	90
1041	08:30	6100	11	125	21	0	0	0:00	0:00	0:03	0:30	87
	09:00		14	121	8	0	0	0:00	0:00	0:00	0:30	94
1041			25	123	14	0	0	0:00	0:00	0:03	1:00	90
			99	83	14	0	1	0:00	0:02	0:57	4:35	89

Intvl

The time frame to which the each part of the data refers.

ACD CALLS

Num Answd: The number of calls answered that have been routed by the ACD.

Avg Talk: This is the average time the agent has spent on each ACD call.

Avg Wait: The time the agent has spent ready and available to take calls, averaged out as time spent waiting between calls.

NON ACD CALLS

Num In: The number of non ACD calls received, such as internal extension dialling.

Num Out: The number of non ACD calls made, such as calling the supervisor.

Time In: The time spent on inbound non ACD calls.

Time Out: The time spent on outbound non ACD calls.

Total Not Ready: The time spent in wrap up, doing after call work.

Time - Logn: The length of time during the specific time frame that the agent has been logged in to the system.

ACD/Logn %: This is the agent occupancy level, including time spent on ACD calls and in wrap up (but not in ready/wait time).

Other useful information which you will find on the daily reports or other special reports:

Log in : Giving you the time agents started work. This helps you to keep a firm eye on punctuality. There will also be a **Log out** report and totals of **Log in** for the day. These can be useful for overtime pay purposes.

Total Calls: Shows the total number of calls, inbound and out-bound handled by each agent, and the daily report should give you the office total.

Avg Wrap: The average time spent on after call work in wrap up.

Take a look at this in conjunction with talk time and average handling time. Some agents prefer to keep callers on the line just a little bit longer while they wrap up and therefore have short wrap up times, but slightly longer talk time and therefore 'normal' handling times.

Short Calls: You would set your own parameters for highlighting short calls - perhaps all calls that are less than your minimum length call. If you don't really get any 'quick' calls, you might set the parameter at 10 seconds or less, for wrong numbers etc.

% Various: These can be misleading. Check out what total the percentages are a part of before you make any assumptions. The key is to ensure you fully understand what the figures represent before using them.

%NAvail: Understand where the system is getting its figures from. The % not available may be from a BUSY or WALKAWAY key, separate to the Wrap Up key which the agents can use for a range of non available time such as comfort breaks, coaching sessions, morning briefings or meetings. Some of this time may be considered productive and some may not.

To try and restrict the use of this key to non productive time may mean using the wrap up key for coaching etc., which will distort your average call handling times or the login/logout key which may ruin your ambitions on using this key for payroll and overtime purposes! Also check whether your ACD automatically logs agents out if they are in BUSY for longer than a set time.

Objectives

There are several objectives in using Agent Data. Firstly, it enables you to create an office average so that you can benchmark each agent and identify their strengths and weaknesses. Your supervisors will want to study this information in depth. Log in times demonstrate punctuality while call handling time can identify training needs. You can also flag possible problems, such as tardiness, long wrap up times, a disproportionate number of comfort breaks etc.

These figures also let you share information with the agents so that they can map their contribution to the company, and feel proud of it. Agent Data is usually supplied in individual, team (or supervisor) and full office reports, plus they can also be defined by queue.

This latter report can be more accurate in evaluating agent performance when the agents are multi-skilled and handling more than one queue. Each queue type may have different average talk or wrap up times which, if not separated out, can distort overall average data.

Call Data

Again, these reports are usually supplied in half hour intervals, hourly intervals, daily, weekly and monthly. You may be able to request specific hours also, from x time to y time. Reports can be supplied showing all calls together, or separated out into specific group/queues.

Your interval report for calls handled by queue may look something

Summarized ACD-DN Performance Interval Report
courtesy of Nortel showing Meridian MAX standard management report

```
                    Summarized ACD-DN Performance Report        Page 1
                               Interval Report

   ABC Corporation              Date: 04/18/95        Time:22:29:08

   Intervals: 08:00 - 12:00 Day: 04/18/95
```

ACD-DN	INTVL	SRV LVL%	AVG DEL SEC	DEL-ANN 1ST	2ND	ANSW	OVFL IN	ABND	ACD TALK SEC	NOT RDY SEC	NON IN SEC	ACD OUT SEC
Day: 04/18/95												
6100	08:00	100	1	2	0	7	0	0	25	1	0	0
	08:30	98	55	106	62	140	0	9	142	20	0	20
	09:00	96	79	153	106	149	0	14	136	28	0	180
	09:30	89	77	178	110	165	0	22	146	36	0	0
	10:00	100	58	142	78	141	0	16	154	56	0	60
	10:30	95	44	104	64	162	0	11	144	41	0	0
	11:00	100	34	90	53	161	0	9	157	43	0	7
	11:30	99	72	136	96	133	0	14	180	41	0	102
	12:00	99	70	137	105	126	0	20	161	42	0	0
6100		97	54	1048	674	1184	0	115	138	38	0	41
6130	08:00	95	1	3	0	6	0	0	29	2	0	0
	08:30	100	56	104	63	143	0	7	147	22	0	22
	09:00	99	75	150	104	151	0	13	140	25	0	175
	09:30	95	78	179	108	160	0	19	150	36	0	5
	10:00	96	59	143	77	143	0	18	155	54	0	0
	10:30	100	43	105	63	159	0	9	169	47	0	15
	11:00	100	30	93	55	160	0	11	165	53	0	8
	11:30	99	66	134	97	134	0	16	157	43	0	69
	12:00	89	70	136	106	127	0	24	158	45	0	28
6130		97	53	1047	673	1183	0	117	141	36	0	35

like the Meridian Max report shown on the previous page and once again, the intervals show the time frame requested for this specific interval report:

QUEUE PROFILE

Srv Lvl%: Having set your desired parameters in the configuration, this system works out your achieved service levels throughout the day.

Avg Del: This is the average speed of answer, the time spent in queue waiting for an agent.

Del-Ann 1st 2nd: This is the number of calls that held in queue and received the first recorded announcement, and those that held and received the second.

NUMBER OF CALLS

Answ: The total number of calls answered.

Ovfl In: This shows the number of calls that time-overflowed into this queue from another.

Abnd: The total number of calls lost.

These reports may or may not give you your service level. In some cases you may need another report to see if you have achieved your goals, and there are one or two systems where you may even need to get your calculator out!

More and more ACD vendors are providing reports which can be fully customised and therefore your chosen service level can be easily configured and shown.

The most important information that you will use is:

NCO: Number of calls offered, the total number of inbound calls which arrived at the ACD. This is one of the crucial sets of data, instrumental in call forecasting and staff scheduling.

NCH: Number of calls handled lets you know how many calls successfully reached an agent. These figures can become more complex when you give your callers the opportunity to use IVR or leave a message on voice mail - are these calls included in call handling, automatic handling or abandoned calls?

Delay before Abandoning Report

courtesy of Nortel showing Meridian MAX standard management report

```
                    ACD-DN Delay Before Abandoning Report         Page 1
                              Daily Report

ABC Corporation              Date: 04/20/95          Time:20:40:12

Days: 04/13/95 - 04/19/95
```

ACD DN	DAY	CALLS ABAND	0- <12	12- <24	24- <36	36- <48	48- <60	60- <120	120- <180	180- <240	240- <300	300- +	AVG DEL SEC	LONG DEL SEC
			---PERCENT OF CALLS ABANDONED WITHIN (SEC)--											
6100	04/14/95	9	67	22	11	0	0	0	0	0	0	0	12	32
	04/17/95	203	22	13	14	7	4	17	8	3	4	1	60	314
	04/18/95	119	29	14	10	10	13	20	4	0	0	0	40	166
	04/19/95	64	36	20	14	8	5	14	3	0	0	0	29	126
6100		395	27	15	13	8	7	17	6	2	2	1	48	314
6200	04/14/95	0	0	0	0	0	0	0	0	0	0	0	0	0
	04/17/95	2	50	0	50	0	0	0	0	0	0	0	19	38
	04/18/95	2	100	0	0	0	0	0	0	0	0	0	0	0
	04/19/95	2	50	50	0	0	0	0	0	0	0	0	9	16
6200		6	66	17	17	0	0	0	0	0	0	0	9	38
6500	04/14/95	0	0	0	0	0	0	0	0	0	0	0	0	0
	04/15/95	0	0	0	0	0	0	0	0	0	0	0	0	0
	04/16/95	0	0	0	0	0	0	0	0	0	0	0	0	0
	04/17/95	0	0	0	0	0	0	0	0	0	0	0	0	0
	04/18/95	0	0	0	0	0	0	0	0	0	0	0	0	0
	04/19/95	0	0	0	0	0	0	0	0	0	0	0	0	0
6500		0	0	0	0	0	0	0	0	0	0	0	0	0
		401	28	15	13	8	6	17	6	1	2	1	47	314

NCL: Number of calls lost or abandoned. There will usually be a report dedicated to abandoned calls such as the Meridian Max report shown above.

These identify the time that callers gave up and put the phone down. Worth studying, this enables you to pinpoint the time where a suitable message might just keep your callers on the line a little bit longer, giving you more time to get to them before they abandon.

Whenever you make a change, record the results over a month and see if you've improved the caller tolerance rate.

Days: Shows the time frame requested.

ACD DN: The identity number of the queue.

Day: Shows each day separately.

Calls Aband: Total number of calls which have abandoned.

Percent of Calls Abandoned within (sec): This shows the percentage of calls which have abandoned within specific time frames, as set by you.

Avg Del: This is the average time a call waited in queue before abandoning.

Long Del: This shows the longest time a call waited in queue before abandoning.

If you can load your ACD data into an Excel programme or similar, you will then be able to produce reports in whatever format you prefer. These reports are something solid that you can share with other departments, particularly sales.

Voice Mail

Just a quick word about Voice Mail. One of its problems is sometimes referred to as "the death spiral" which is a pretty gruesome name. This is due to the impact Voice Mail can have on your call reports.

If for example you have an unusual day with greater call volume than anticipated, more callers may ask the system to transfer them to voice mail to leave messages, rather than continue holding. As these messages are usually brief they can distort the average call handling figures. If this continues you may assume that your average handling time has reduced and using Erlang tables decide to lower your staffing levels.

This creates a vicious circle where more callers choose to go to Voice Mail and the average handling time reduces yet further. Taken to a ridiculous extreme the end result is a call centre staffed only with Voice Mail boxes.

There is another problem associated with Voice Mail when it is used to offer call backs. If your work load is particularly high, your agents are struggling to handle the volume and you anticipate this continuing for the day, there is little point in advising customers that you will call them back, if you don't have any agents to perform that task. The end result is customers may call back again, further increasing the work load and you end up with even poorer customer service.

Real Time Reports

Real-time reports can also be printed off, but most of the time these are used on screen to keep a check on the present situation. However well you have forecasted your calls and organised your staff rosters, there will always be unexpected situations that were not planned. Absenteeism is one you cannot control, but an advertising campaign placed by the marketing department is one you should be able to!

The most important aspect of real time management is maintaining good service *quality*. It is so easy to abandon good practice when faced with service levels crashing through the floor. Because the achievement of a desired service level is given such emphasis, the natural inclination of supervisors is to encourage agents to rush calls when service levels are threatened. Unfortunately if you offer poor service you are likely to spend more time on repeat calls and sorting out problems which will have a much worse impact on service levels.

This situation can also cause planning headaches as call handling times reduce as a result of agents rushing their calls and perhaps postponing some after call work. The data for the day will distort your future call forecasting and staff scheduling.

The key to managing is to ensure that during unexpected peaks all contingencies for peak traffic have been utilised. This means a workable escalation plan should be developed before a crisis happens.

Escalation Plan

Many call centres use a tiered approach.

The first level is designed to help short, immediate problems. Make sure every available body that can take calls is transferred from any admin. work back to the phones. Those agents normally assigned to outbound, data-entry or correspondence can become splendid reinforcements.

The next level depends upon your own circumstances and could include:

• Reassigning or overflowing agents from other answer groups.

- Pull in volunteers from other departments - obviously the practicalities will depend upon the complexity of the call handling

- Meetings and training can be postponed.

- Intraflow calls to a service agency.

- Offer overtime. If the agents understand how important each individual is and therefore the huge difference just one person can make to poor service levels, you may be able to persuade call outs and overtime.

- Use your messaging system to advise of delays, and the reason why if known, and give your callers a choice of using voice mail boxes or call back facilities. You could advise extended opening hours and encourage callers to ring back during that period.

If agents are trained in queue behaviour, clearly understand the importance of adhering to schedules and in the principal of quality above service levels, they will then know how to react in such a situation.

You may also have unexpected troughs and the opposite of the above can be used. You could place additional people on admin. work, outbound, data-entry or correspondence. See if other departments need extra help. Use the time effectively for activities you have always wanted to do, but never had the time, such as special brain storming sessions, idea creation schemes and instigate some ad hoc training. Offer TOIL (time off in lieu) - *unpaid time off* - you will be amazed at the number of people that will want to take advantage of this.

Handling each call accurately and with quality service should always take precedence over service levels and as long as you have ensured everything possible has been done to provide additional resources, the only difficult part remaining is ensuring senior management understand this!

Historical information

The historical reports can be generated through the day to give an indication of what is going on now and these can be used to detect trends. As we know, the service level is a primary focus in call centre planning. This information can never be offered dynamically in the strictest sense, as it has to look back at a number of calls and/or an amount of time in order to make the calculation.

The same applies to average speed of answer and average time to abandonment where the system has to look back.

Real time information

On the screen the number of calls in queue is dynamic, as is longest current wait, and current agent status. You therefore can see some contradictions where there are no calls waiting in queue but your screen shows a service level of 82% in 20 seconds and likewise it may show 98% service level but the queues are full of waiting calls.

As calls are random, it only takes a few seconds for them to spiral out of control but because the service level is looking back at the last ten minutes, it won't reflect those new developments immediately. Trends can start to develop under your nose.

Therefore, real time management needs to prioritise the number of calls in queue and the longest wait, before the service level shown on screen. Agent status, which becomes the primary focus if an unfavourable trend is identified should be looked at next.

If you start to notice unusual call volumes early in the shift, and you wish to assume that this trend will continue throughout the day, you can perform these mathematical calculations to see whether you need to activate a contingency plan and pull some extra staff in.

Take a look at your normal daily traffic patterns and work out the percentage of the day's calls you would expect to have received by this time of day. Perhaps by 12 noon it is 55%. Simply take the calls received since opening and divide by this percentage, then multiply by 100. You have now calculated the number of calls you might expect to receive today, if this trend continues. You can then break this down further to work out how many calls you might expect in each half hour segment.

It is the moment by moment decisions you make that will help you to maintain your service levels and the planning and procedures you have in place with specific details of when and how to activate your escalation plan.

To conclude:

- establish an achievable service level
- forecast your call traffic
- calculate staffing levels
- develop your contingency escalation procedures
- plan and manage non-phone activities
- organise schedules that match the number of agents with the workload as closely as possible

Easy!

Let's take a look at some of the technology around that can help you do all this.

CHAPTER 3: TECHNOLOGY

In the 1990s we have seen an explosion in call centre technology. You can buy hardware and software to automate just about anything and everything you want. They won't necessarily work together though!

For the new call centre manager, the technology available is overwhelming and the technobabble often incomprehensible. This chapter attempts to translate the jargon into plain English and identify the benefits and applications available today.

What is really needed and what is simply nice to have?

Technology should be regarded as an enabler, helping your employees to do their jobs effectively. In any purchasing decision, your business needs and your customer requirements should be the key drivers.

I shall start with the most crucial piece of technology in the call centre - the ACD.

3a: The Automatic Call Distributor (ACD)

Whether or not you bother with anything else, the ACD is the heart of the inbound call centre, pumping incoming calls to wherever they need to go. The ACD is synonymous with the call centre.

The early ACDs simply distributed calls evenly and equitably to all the agents available. Nowadays, they are much more sophisticated and can be configured with a variety of different parameters based on different services, priorities and skills.

People dial your number, the call arrives via the exchange at your ACD and the ACD then tells that call exactly where it needs to go - this could be the first available agent, or the first who can speak French, or it may need to hold the call in queue, play it music and messages *"We are sorry, there are no agents available at the moment but please stay on the line and we will be with you shortly"*.

The more sophisticated ACDs can take a look at the status of other call centres you may have networked and decide whether to keep the call at the local ACD or send it to another.

You set the parameters from which the ACD makes all its decisions.

It is a 'no brainer' decision to purchase (or rent) a system with call distribution facilities for your new call centre, but it is a very complex one as to which you choose.

Ranging from several thousand pounds to millions, your choice will depend on your anticipated call volume, how you want to distribute calls in your call centre today and the functionality you anticipate you may need tomorrow. With such a tremendous evolution in technology, future-proofing has been difficult to obtain.

ACD evolution

If we take a look at the evolution of the ACD, the first type of call distributor was available in the 1960s,supplied by Bell System and used by the airlines. The first stand-alone ACD was developed by Collins Radio (now part of Rockwell) for Continental Airlines in 1973.

Soon after this, Datapoint introduced the Infoswitch ACD, still used by many call centres today. In the mid to late 1970s PBX manufacturers in the U.S. introduced ACD capabilities into their telephone switches (sometimes called hybrids) including AT&T and Northern Telecom (now NORTEL).

The 1980s saw the introduction of more stand alone ACDs such as the Aspect for the large call centres and the STS for the small call centre. However it was not until the late 80s and early 1990s that ACDs for the smaller call centre really took off with systems like the SDX. The 1990s have also seen the creation of network based systems from the major network providers (PTOs), called Centrex services.

By the mid 90s the development of call distribution by outbound diallers enabling true blending has resulted in the traditional ACDs now offering power or predictive dialler capabilities. The features gap between the systems is becoming progressively smaller. In addition there has been the introduction of the PC based ACD, sometimes called Soft ACD or Adjunct Processor.

ACD Programming

If we take a look at a typical ACD, you will start to understand the enormous capabilities of these machines. However, the skill lies in configuring the system so that its capabilities are optimised for your individual call centre. Everything the ACD chooses to do has been pre-programmed by you.

Calls arrive at your ACD. The ACD can recognise and differentiate calls from the number the caller has dialled and can therefore handle these differently. (It needs computer telephony integration to recognise the number the caller has dialled from - see CTI.) It checks the availability of suitable agents. Perhaps you want certain calls to be handled by a special group of people, or just one person. If there is an agent free it will send the call to that agent and the agent's telephone turret (or screen) will advise the agent from where the call has come.

For example, callers dialling in from France and Germany can be identified by the number called and routed to those agents who speak French and German. The agent's phone or screen will let them know which country so that they can answer the call in the appropriate language.

This can also be helpful for centralised offices handling both customer service and sales. If the general public are given different numbers to call, they can be identified and treated differently.

Priorities

Inbound calls can also be given different priorities. If all agents are busy and calls are holding for both general enquiries and sales, you may wish to give priority to sales rather than handle them in the order they arrived at the switch. If you offer toll free numbers throughout Europe, you may wish to give priority to the most expensive calls to reduce your phone bills.

The priorities for calls held in queue can be handled in many different ways as can agent groups. Some ACDs allow agents to handle multiple queues, others don't which can be restrictive, particularly to the smaller call centre.

Music & Messaging

When no agent is free, the ACD may intercept the call as it rings out and play the caller a message. This might be just the 'all agents are busy, please hold' type message that we have become used to, or it may be something much more sophisticated and offer the caller different options. These might be leaving a message in voice mail, requesting a call back, or faxing information.

Message playing can differ considerably between ACDs. You may want all your callers to hear a message after a 30 second wait, but if your message is already playing when that parameter is reached, callers may have to wait much longer until the message has finished and can be replayed again.

Others may cut your caller into the message at the time specified, but this could be half way through or near the end of the message. Multiple announcement machines offer multiple start times.

After another set period of time you may want to play another message. We are used to hearing, 'sorry all agents are still busy, but please stay on the line and one will be with you shortly.' If you use the ACD to supply this message you can purchase as many as you like, but this can be very expensive. For each message you may require a RAN (recorded announcements) trunk card. Alternatively, music and messaging has become an art with companies offering a variety of services, which are more flexible and possibly work out more cost effective. These are all designed to tempt the caller to stay longer on the line.

Auto answering

Once an agent is free, the call is usually 'forced'. In other words, auto answering where the agent, who would normally wear a head-set, receives the call automatically and the call is announced by a short, light bleep in the ear. Surprisingly, these bleeps are not intrusive.

Their telephone turret or screen will show where the call has come from (if known) so the agent is able to answer appropriately. If the agent needs to contact the supervisor, they can place the caller on hold and usually use a 'hot key' direct to their supervisor. Alternatively they may need to transfer the call. Most ACDs now allow you to transfer a call to a queue, rather than a specific agent.

Supervisor monitoring

Meanwhile, the supervisor should be able to monitor any call, listening in without the caller being aware. This practice is not accepted globally. Whilst some countries use this method freely for quality control and training purposes, other countries have prohibited or restricted its use as an infringement of privacy.

Recording

Other features might include some kind of emergency button. Call recorders can be added to ACDs and these can be as simple as a dictaphone tape recorder to a highly sophisticated system which records each and every call and has a tracking device to enable the supervisor to find specific recordings quickly and easily.

Again, call recording is used extensively in some countries for coaching purposes, and is banned in others.

Wrap up

Each agent's telephone turret has a key for wrap up which prevents further calls reaching the agent until they are ready. As we have seen, wrap up time is vital in assessing call handling time and this button should only be used for that purpose.

Activity codes

There may also be an activity code button, used extensively by some companies to help determine the type of calls received. The agent would normally select this button and input a particular code. The ACD may default to a code of your choice but the system cannot differentiate between an agent purposefully not entering a code and an agent who simply forgets.

Night messaging or diversion

If you are not a 24 hour operation, when closed you can choose to have a night message played, or divert calls to an answer bureau, or even to another call centre. There are several examples of global companies who send their calls from one continent to another in a 'follow the sun' strategy.

Management Information Reports

Other than call distribution, the ACD's value comes with the reports it offers you. As we have seen in the previous chapter, you can evaluate just about every piece of data you can think of, from individual agent performance to abandoned call trends. Whilst many ACDs offer standard reports, most now enable you to customise reports to whatever you want to show.

The screen information provided by the ACD, as also shown in the last chapter, is vital for daily call centre management. Supervisors are able to monitor call volume and respond to situations (remember calls are random), making dynamic changes and ensuring service levels are protected.

Wallboards

Electronic displays, such as wallboards, can be used to show the agents the status of queues or to provide information throughout the day or motivational messages. These are sometimes provided with the ACD and sometimes need to be purchased separately.

Many ACDs now offer automatic outbound dialling capabilities which are detailed in the next section.

So how do you go about selecting what is right for you? These systems are the largest item of capital expenditure you are likely to make and so errors are costly.

Let's first take a look at some of the systems available today.

Stand alone ACDs

As their name implies, their sole purpose is call distribution. These usually provide faster call handling, are more flexible with regards to call routing and integration with other call centre applications and are highly focused on automatic call distribution. However, they are often more expensive, some do not support analogue or provide PBX functionality restricting call transfers to your administrative system,so requiring tie lines - dedicated lines between the two systems.

Companies selecting stand alone are *more likely* to be larger centres that may wish to network to other centres.

Hybrid ACDs

PBX based ACDs offer functionality to both the call centre and administration, with call distribution and switchboard working together. They may not have all the features of the stand alone or the processing power but are generally less expensive. Small and large call centres can find these advantageous, and some may have equally good networking capability as stand alones.

Soft ACDs

Comparatively inexpensive for the smaller call centre, everything is PC based so these systems can provide exceptional functionality with latest technology including CTI as standard. They are very new in the market and some fear is expressed over the robustness of these systems.

Probably only addressing the smaller marketplace at this time. As confidence in these systems grows, their market could expand considerably. These are sometimes called Adjunct Processors or PC Based ACDs.

Centrex Services

This is where ACD functionality is 'leased' from your network provider and housed at the public exchange. The main advantage is no capital outlay, although many ACD vendors are now leasing systems.

With centrex you have built in future proofing, and don't require the space or power facilities required for an on site system. Centrex may not be available everywhere and there are control issues. Obviously there is also the long term cost to take into consideration. See the later section which details services available through Centrex.

So how to choose which call distribution system? Perhaps the easiest way is to use a good call centre consultant and our industry is blessed with some exceptionally good independent companies. You will still need to have some awareness of your needs, and of course you may not have the budget to include consultant services.

As with any product, before you make your selection you need to know what you want the product to achieve. List your primary needs, and that will reduce the players on the field straight away:

- maximum number of anticipated agents (and double it)

- maximum number of exchange lines

- one site or multi-site and networked

- number of different queue types (calls you want to treat differently or have separate data available on them)

- number of different agent groups (for each different type of queue answering you may need a different agent skill group to respond)

- number of different intercept announcements (for each different queue type, different language?)

- reports required (sounds silly but if you need more copies of reports than the ACD can schedule, you have a time consuming problem)

- types of software application you desire (see next sections)

- outbound functionality required

- maintenance services required

- budget available

Once you have got past these basics, you can take a closer look at the players you have left. This is a good time to think about site visits. The easiest option is to ask the ACD vendors to arrange site visits for you, but remember they will select their happiest customers. If you can also arrange visits through an impartial third party, you may make other discoveries. See how each company is using their system and what they find is the most important tool. Always ask what they wish the system could do but can't.

In order to get an actual price, you will need to list your requirements. You will need to make decisions on numbers before you put your tender out to purchase or lease your ACD.

1   Number of agent positions needed to be fully equipped

2   Maximum number of agent positions, incorporating 2-5 years growth

3   Number of supervisor positions

4   Number of analogue lines

5   Number of digital lines, including ISDN/DASSII

6   Private networks, or VPNs

7   Number of master screens (for major systems administration)

8   Number of Supervisor screens (for daily monitoring)

9   Number of printers

10   Number of wallboards (electronic displays)

11   Number and type of telephone turrets and handsets

12   Number of headsets

13   Number of recorded announcements

14   Recording facilities - what is required

15   UPS - uninterruptable power supply/generator/battery back up

In addition the pricing should detail the following:

a   *CTI features itemised and costings itemised*

b   *Automated outbound dialling capabilities and costings*

c   *IVR and/or auto attendant features/capabilities and costings* d   *Additional applications available such as workforce management software, scripting software, top and tail recording capabilities*

e   *Cabling to all equipment*

f   *Your required maintenance cover with response times*

g   *Cost of ongoing maintenance in subsequent years*

h   *Remote diagnostic capabilities*

i   *Any sub contracting*

j   *Training in system administration*

k   *Training for supervisors to use ACD*

l   *Training for all employees to use telephone turrets*

m   *Training in the support systems*

n   *Ongoing training costs for new supervisors etc.*

o   *Manuals and guides (how many)*

Once you have received your tenders, you should be able to see clearly what each ACD vendor can offer you and at what price.

You will also need to consider your workplace.

ACDs need to have their own space and are usually kept in a secure room. If you are purchasing or leasing an ACD you will want to identify a corner to house it, and the room needs to be designed to incorporate enough power sockets and perhaps be large enough for the system administrators master screen.

Check if your chosen ACD needs air conditioning, and if so ensure the unit is not placed directly above the ACD cabinet! You may also want to put a phone extension in the mains room alongside the ACD. If something does go wrong you may find yourself running between the mains room and a telephone in order to try and assess the problem!

Make sure your wiring is flood proofed and the mains room has as many contingencies to protect from flood and fire as possible. Remember the ACD is the heart of the call centre, and any interruption to service is always serious.

3b: Centrex services

At this stage you might consider Centrex which in basic terms means that the functionality of the ACD has been moved into the network, away from your company's building. It is not available world-wide so check first to see if you have that option open to you.

Centrex was first introduced into the market as a service, independent of technology. It aimed to offer four innovative and unique services:

- Direct inward dial to any line (DDI or DID)

- Itemised long distance by line

- Itemised equipment billing by line

- Multi-location termination within the Centrex, serving an area without mileage charges

With development and deregulation of the telecommunications industry, the first three are now widely available, however serving multi-location organisations is not yet available by other forms of call distribution.

As Centrex shares resources between customers, it can lower costs and offer greater flexibility. For example, customers enjoy a 24 hour maintenance cover, they have automatic future proofing and have a one stop shop for most of their call centre applications. As the system is a 'pay as you go', you can increase or decrease capacity quickly and easily - ideal if you have major peaks and troughs.

It is generally considered that Centrex does minimise the amount of blocking that occurs when there are not enough ACD lines to cope with the number of calls arriving at the switch.

Centrex offers similar functionality to any ACD. You can have music and messaging, IVR, predictive dialling, intelligent routing and CTI to enable screen popping and simultaneous exchange of voice and data (transferring both the call and the screen information at the same time).

One disadvantage is that MIS reports that can be generated from the Centrex do not always meet management requirements exactly and customisation may not be possible.

The on-going costs are also a major factor.

Organisations that have multiple sites, spread geographically and require continually changing call handling requirements are most likely to benefit from Centrex, if indeed it is available to you in the first place.

Once you have selected your choice of call distribution, you now need to perform the most intricate part of call centre management - configuring the system to your individual requirements. You'll find this under project management.

3c: Diallers

A telephone call is the only media which allows real-time interactive communications and hence is invaluable in problem solving. It is universally available and immediate. It also provides a sales channel which is considerably cheaper than face to face field sales.

Thus outbound dialling is becoming more and more popular for debt collecting and telemarketing.

However, outbound dialling is very labour intensive. It starts with deciding who to call, and when best to call. Business customers need to be contacted during the day, but residential customers might be more accessible in the evenings. Agents then need to access the database, dial and wait for the connection. At this point they may find the phone engaged, or on answerphone. It may be the wrong number, unobtainable or a fax line, or it may simply ring out unanswered. Surveys show that only approximately 50% of calls will actually connect to a person.

Manual dialling is therefore considered to be inefficient and costly. It is also very demoralising for the agents, whose time is constantly being wasted.

Generically known as Power Diallers, automatic outbound dialling systems can increase efficiency by up to 300%. They range from software starting at around £1000 to sophisticated systems costing in the region of £250K for 25 operators.

Power dialling methods can be defined as follows:

- **Manual dialling** via the keyboard of a number displayed on the PC screen

- **Screen dialling** by selecting the number on the screen using a mouse to point and click

- **Preview dialling** uses screens of data downloaded from a central database. The agent then initiates the call usually by using a pre-programmed button on the keyboard, or screen.

- **Power dialling** takes this one step further. The system dials as many calls as it has lines available and, using answer detect, puts through live calls to agents. The system identifies network tones such as ringing, engaged, unobtainable, faxphones and answerphones and filters these out. At the same time, the data about the called party is popped onto the screen to allow the agent to start the call in a meaningful way.

Agent productivity is increased dramatically, by as much as 300%, but there is a drawback. It does not check first to see if an agent is available to take the call and the Power Dialler therefore just hangs up when it finds no agent is free. The person who has just answered the call finds the line goes dead - a nuisance call. For this reason, true Power diallers are not favoured. To overcome the nuisance call problem, further technology is available.

- **Predictive dialling** uses a pacing algorithm (mathematical formula) which regulates the number of outbound calls made based on the probability of an agent being available. The likelihood of nuisance calls being made is greatly reduced. Predictive dialling also relies on a consistent average call handling time so that predicting when to place the next call is more reliable.

- **Progressive dialling** goes one stage further and actually monitors the status of operators before calls are made. This is probably the most efficient form of Power dialling as it keeps the operators supplied with live calls and virtually eliminates nuisance calls.

These systems automate the process of dialling out and eliminate those frustrating errors made on the keypad which can only be rectified by starting again from scratch. They also take appropriate action with calls once their status has been identified. Those with no reply or engaged tones can be rescheduled for later in the day, and those with unobtainable or fax tones can be tagged for checking.

Call blending

Whilst stand alone outbound dialling systems have been widely used by companies with dedicated outbound agents handling substantial lists, there is now a move towards call blending.

This is where agents are skilled in both inbound and outbound and when required can 'switch' between the two during the course of the day. The stand alone systems can now be purchased with inbound call distribution capabilities, whilst ACDs can now be purchased with predictive dialling functionality.

The beauty of this is that it allows you to capture substantial amounts of agent 'ready time' and put that time to use on outbound calling campaigns. Inbound agents can spend a lot of time waiting for calls to come in and it can be a frustrating sight watching a group of agents standing ready with nothing to do for a long time. It is just as frustrating for the agents themselves, making the day long and tedious. But to meet customer service levels dictated by today's competitive pressures, you may need to overstaff for those difficult-to-predict peak periods.

Therefore the circumstances in which you might wish to have some kind of automatic outbound dialling facility, or at least to blend your inbound and outbound calls are to improve your agent productivity when you have very high peaks and very low troughs where staffing cannot be scheduled easily. However such diallers do require a huge list of at least 500 names to contact. The gains of 300% sometimes quoted are generally when lists are larger than this, with a least 6 agents dedicated to outbound calling.

You might use outbound dialling to make welcome calls to resolve any teething problems with new purchases, which could also prevent a later inbound call. Or to contact existing customers and make sure they are satisfied. The call can be used to try and cross sell or upsell. Calling customers about late payment has proved to be more productive than sending reminder letters so debt collection is very popular. It is also a way of addressing financial difficulties with customers and working out a payment process which is acceptable to both your company and the customer. If you do have excessive peak periods, offer a call back system which your customers may be grateful for.

Database integration

However, integrating an outbound strategy is a little more complex than simply choosing whether to purchase an automated dialler or an ACD with outbound facilities. Moving to automated dialling might well involve further process changes at the same time, particularly with data integration. Can you get real time access to your customer records fast enough? If not, will a copy of the record made overnight be sufficiently up to date for the application in mind? Once the outbound call is made, how do you update the customer record to maintain the audit trail?

To give an example, if you consider implementing an outbound campaign for late payments, it's vital that if a customer's cheque arrives that morning, or the customer calls to discuss the problem, then that 'target' is removed from the calling list. Whilst this sounds simple, the technology solution may not be.

Data integrity and an audit trail of changes is vital and this complicates any write access to systems. A front end system managing customer contacts may well help with this problem, by capturing and storing results of calls. However the more information an agent needs to put back into the system will generally require more complex integration and development during implementation. Trying to automate this process is fraught with issues, not least being the system development required to achieve it.

The data required for the lists may also be spread across several systems. A typical problem may be that the data required to define who to contact resides in the marketing database but the information required by the agent for the call is housed in the billing database. This means data consolidation, and often requires a third system to make the other two talk to each other.

Considerable thought also needs to be given to your agents who will need significant training and possible incentives if they are to handle both inbound and outbound calls.

The plus side is that you have a more manageable call centre. Remember inbound calls are random and anything you can do to increase staffing during peaks and decrease staffing during troughs results in higher productivity. Call blending does just this, moving agents from outbound mode to inbound mode when call arrival starts to peak.

But of course it is only an option if your company will gain benefit from making a substantial amount of outbound calls.

3d: Computer Telephony Integration(CTI)

In simple terms, CTI is simply where the computer and the telephone talk to teach other and give each other information or instructions. There are several books available on CTI which cover the topic in great detail, such as 'Computer Telephone Integration' by Rob Walters and this section only serves to give you a taste of CTI and the benefits it can bring to your business.

The most primitive forms of Computer Telephony Integration started by simply joining the computer to the telephone through the use of a device called a modem. This meant people could buy software which would enable them to send faxes from their computers, use their computers to dial out rather than pick up the telephone handset and even get their computers to take email messages for them. Point and click, the modem dials the requested number, and you are connected.

Protocols

The physical link between the PC and the telephone system consists of a piece of wire and a language, called a *protocol*, which they use to communicate with each other. Unfortunately, every telephone system uses a different protocol. Thus you need a translater. This is an *API* - an Application Programme Interface.

APIs

Rufus Grig, a renowned specialist in CTI, once used the analogy of cars to describe this interface. Different manufacturers make cars in different ways. A diesel engine works in a very different way to a petrol engine. Front wheel drive differs from rear wheel drive, some cars have turbo charges fitted etc.

However, the 'interface' that the driver sees remains pretty much the same from car to car. Steering wheels, gears, brakes and accelerators work the same way. Without exception, the brake and the accelerator are always used by the right foot, and the brake pedal is always found on the left of the accelerator pedal.

By and large, any driver can get in any car and drive it away within minutes. There are some variants such as cars with automatic gears. Drivers taught only on this simpler interface are not able to drive the more complex cars with manual gears.

The principle of CTI is the same. Each link works differently but each has an interface - an API.

In order to marry the telephone with the computer, you need a wedding. The number of people you want to use CTI will normally (but not necessarily) dictate whether you have a simple ceremony for just a few guests, or a society event for everyone you know.

These are called first party (or desktop) and third party (or host/server) CTI. I have no idea what happened to second party. If you find out, please do let me know! Although the terms desktop and host are much more descriptive, I will refer to them as first and third party as this seems to be how the majority of people and vendors discuss them.

First party CTI (desktop)

First party CTI sits in the PC and allows one PC to behave as if it's your telephone extension. It only knows what is happening on your own telephone and therefore is beneficial for personal applications such as desktop contact management packages and personal organisers. It will happily talk to your host database and can offer a multitude of functionality - but only to that one PC.

However, by purchasing first party CTI you can take advantage of a small pilot programme before you commit to major expenditure. You can monitor the success of the system and evaluate its benefits. In addition, you have the flexibility of adding as many extra seats as you want, when you want and can restrict the use to as many or as few agents as you wish.

 First party CTI requires a type of wedding such as *TAPI* - Telephone Applications Programming Interface. This is a software programme promoted by Microsoft.

Third Party CTI (server/host)

Third party CTI resides in the server so you buy one package which can be accessed and enjoyed by everyone on the network. It is therefore much more expensive than first party (depending upon the number of agents you want to use it). This type of CTI requires the type of marriage ceremony provided by *TSAPI*, Telephone Server Applications Programming Interface, a piece of software promoted by Novell.

Remember the S in TSAPI is for server and then you can't go wrong.

There are currently three APIs in popular use, each developed by one of the three main computer companies, Novell and Microsoft with the third being IBM and their product, Callpath.

A programme that supports TAPI would be known as 'TAPI Compliant' - it complies with the standards laid down by the creators of TAPI.

The war between the various APIs for market dominance has similarities to the VHF and BETA MAX video wars in the 70s, but I personally believe there is room for all of them. Many applications are now marketing themselves as both TAPI and TSAPI compliant so the customer does not need to make a costly choice when purchasing other software. That never happened with video recorders.

If you hear the term *CSTA,* this stands for Computer Supported Telephony Applications, which is the protocol (language) used between computers and telephone systems, set to a specific standard by ECMA, the European Computer Manufacturers' Association. TAPI, Callpath and TSAPI are all CSTAs.

The industry does enjoy making up more and more buzzwords and acronyms!

Becoming more affordable

Introduced a couple of years ago as a highly expensive application, month after month CTI becomes more affordable, particularly first party. It is generally assumed that call centres purchase third party CTI due to the high volume of users. However, with the increasing drop in price for first party CTI, and the flexibility it affords, that assumption has become flawed.

There is no doubt that third party CTI will continue to address the top end of the CTI marketplace and will continue to attract a premium price from companies who require tailored applications. First party CTI, on the other hand, is able to address a much wider market, bringing off the shelf packaged applications to companies who do not need a bespoke approach.

CTI opens up a whole new world of benefits.

Shaving seconds off the average call handling time can make a huge impact on large call centres, and increase the efficiency of smaller centres.

Calling line identity

A major use of CTI is to automate time-consuming, non productive elements of a call, inbound or outbound. A call comes into the ACD, and the CTI link (whether it sits in the server or at the desktop) looks at the number dialled and/or the number called from (*calling line identity - CLI*) and interrogates the database to see what information is available on that number.

Magic when it works!

CLI is not yet universally available. First, the call must have been initiated on a network belonging to a carrier that supports CLI and at this time there are more that don't than do. The majority of mobile phones don't support CLI either so if your customer is calling you whilst on the road, the CTI link will not be able to identify him.

In some countries the customer may be able to use a special code which inhibits the transmission of his number, because he doesn't want you to know who he is. Or he may be dialling from a company that has DDI and therefore the number that reaches your system is only the generic switchboard number. In this case the CTI link might pull up a list of people that it recognises as using that number. If the customer calls from someone else's premises, then obviously the CTI link won't help.

Of course you may not have the caller's details in your database, so once again no information will appear on screen.

CLI only works when the *number dialled from* is transmitted, exists in your database, and can offer a correct match with one name.

Screen popping

If the database recognises either the number dialled or the number dialled from, it can then pop relevant information onto the screen of the agent who then receives the call. Called s*creen popping,* this is the most desired function of CTI. The agent has no need to ask the caller for their details and this alone can reduce the length of call by typically 15 - 30 seconds. It not only increases agent productivity but enhances customer service too.

For example, take a 50 agent call centre and say each agent handles 120 calls per day with an average handling time of 3 minutes.

20 seconds of each call is spent on asking the caller for their name, or customer number and then accessing the host database to pull the appropriate details onto the screen.

By eliminating this time, each agent can potentially save 40 minutes per day, or 3.33 hours per working week, an 11% increase in productivity.

With 50 agents, this equates to a saving of 166 hours or 22 man days per week, giving you all that extra manpower.

Then, if the agent needs to transfer the call to someone else, the CTI link can send both the call (voice) and the on-screen information (data) together. A huge customer service benefit and time saver, the caller no longer has to repeat the whole story again. The agent to whom the call has been transferred can say, "Ah, Mrs Smith, I see you are having trouble with your widget, let me see if I can help sort this out for you." The agent can take control straight away and give excellent customer service.

Outbound dialling

With first party CTI you can also have screen-based telephony where you point and click at a telephone number on screen and your PC will dial that number for you, *preview dialling*, saving time and reducing misdial errors. Third party CTI, because it resides in the server is able to view everything everyone else is doing, and so can provide you with predictive dialling.

CTI can also be instrumental in offering additional services to the customer such as sending information via fax and IVR.

3e: Voice Processing

Voice processing is defined as the digital storage of the human voice on computer disk. However, unlike data it demands huge amounts of disk space and therefore has only recently become readily available due to the increasing size and falling cost of hard disks.

Voice processing is simply a generic term for a variety of applications which process voice transactions automatically. It enables the call centre to automate tedious transactions, to provide a 24 hour service to customers who might otherwise have to call back the next day, to handle overflow calls at peak times, and to give a personalised service to your regular callers.

IVR

Interactive Voice Response (IVR), is one of these applications which must have CTI to function. IVR is where the caller is answered by a recorded message asking for a numeric response to specific questions or statements. If the caller has a touch tone phone he is able to drive the system by pressing buttons on the telephone keypad. The tones are recognised by the voice processing system which tells the computer what to do. This may result in taking the call to an extension or voice mail box, or to get information from the database which is then spoken back (through voice synthesis) over the phone. A script guides the caller through a menu of information, each time waiting for the caller's response, then reacting accordingly.

An obvious example of an IVR application is telephone banking where customers can make a call, are answered by a recording, they input their personal identification number and are then able to receive information about their account with no live agent involved. Any application which requires remote access to stored data would be suitable for IVR. These could include stocks and parts ordering, student registrations, insurance quotations, flight enquiries and appointment setting.

Speech recognition

For those callers who do not have touch tone telephones, voice or *speech recognition* can be used. The caller is asked to state clearly the extension number or the name of the person they wish to speak with over the telephone line. The voice processing system recognises the words and processes the call accordingly. Simpler systems may just require the caller to say yes or to remain silent.

Speech recognition is a rapidly expanding field and the number of words that can be identified is increasing. Today, it is a simple matter to recognise numbers 0 - 10, key words such as yes and no, a list of specific names and even the letters of the alphabet. It will not be many years before voice processing systems will be able to recognise a couple of thousand words of continuous speech, regardless of accent or pitch and that will make voice response systems even more powerful. Major users of this technology are directory enquiries.

IVR can really make a huge difference for the call centre agents themselves. It can take away the really mundane and repetitive tasks, for example looking up bank balances, leaving the agents with the more interesting and demanding work.

There are times, however when the caller will want to transfer to an agent, to query the information given through the IVR system or because they need information not available on the system. Therefore these voice processing systems should always have a back up enabling callers to press a number (say 0) at any time if they want to cut through the system and speak with a live agent.

At this point the IVR system will contact the call centre, and before putting the caller through it will either whisper the caller's account number in the agent's headset, or will screen pop the caller's information.

Topping & Tailing

Topping and tailing calls is yet another fabulous application for the call centre. Saying, "Good day this is John, how may I help you" a hundred times a day, trying to sound fresh and enthusiastic every time is not always easy.

Topping enables the agent to pre-record his or her greeting which is automatically played as soon as the call routing function has selected an available agent. This recording is made as the caller's details are being popped onto the screen, giving the agent a few seconds to assimilate the information.

Likewise, saying, "Good-bye, and thank you for calling" can be equally tedious. A similar recording can be made to 'tail' the call.

During the course of any conversation, if repetitive information regularly needs to be given, such as terms and conditions, or regulations, a recording can be played. At no time is the caller aware that these are recordings and not live conversation.

The recordings can be sensitive to time, changing from "Good morning" to "Good afternoon" at 12 noon, and be sensitive to CLI or DDI, thus calls from another country would be automatically greeted in the appropriate language, from the various recordings made by your multi-lingual agent.

Auto attendants

In the PBX world, a*uto attendants* enable callers to enter an extension or departmental number and route themselves around an organisation without the need for a live switchboard operator.

Voice mail

Voice mail is a voice processing application familiar to most people. Its primary purpose is the same as an answerphone, enabling a caller to leave a message. However, whereas all the answering machine can do is record messages and play them back, voice mail is far more sophisticated.

It enables the recipient to handle a voice message in the same way as a paper one. The message can be reviewed, copied, stored, annotated, forwarded to one or more people with or without comments. It can also advise recipients that a message is waiting by a variety of methods including lighting a message waiting lamp, ringing an extension or external phone or even a message pager.

Within the context of the call centre, voice mail can offer extra value.

At peak times callers on hold can be offered the choice of leaving a message, in which case they can be put through to a voice mail box. Supervisors can forward a message on to all agents in one hit, advising them of a change in product or service.

Audiotex

Voice processing also includes *audiotex* which is the storage of spoken information for later retrieval through a touch-tone telephone. It first gained notoriety from its use in 'adult entertainment' on premium rate telephone lines. It is an ideal vehicle to use for highly repetitive information such as time-tables, weather reports or sports results, where no interaction with the caller is required.

 It can be used internally to offer a variety of automated services to staff, such as information on canteen menus, career opportunities etc.

Voice forms

Likewise, *voice forms* offer a similar service but these are used to receive information, rather than give information. This is neither a simple answerphone, nor voice mail. The system asks the caller to answer a question and awaits their response before asking the next question. In this way the organisation receives the information it needs in the order in which it is required. Call centre agents can transfer callers who are simply requesting literature to the voice form to capture their names and addresses.

Audio typists can use touch-tone foot pedals to transcribe the stored information at a later time.

There are still more voice processing applications but these are not generally used in a call centre environment.

3f: Workforce management software

Balancing your service levels means matching your staffing to your inbound call flow as best you can.

There are many packages on the market which will do this for you, calculating the number of staff required at any given time.

They work this way. They collect information from the ACD and build a model of your call volume. They quickly assess call patterns throughout the day, week and month and use this to forecast calls for the remainder of the year.

However, to begin with you do need to input much of the data yourself. The system needs to know your operating hours, agent shift patterns, breaks, lunches, scheduled training, briefings, meetings etc. The software then provides you with a complete workforce schedule covering all the different parameters you have entered so you are able to see who should be going for a break and when.

During the course of that schedule, the system learns from what it has forecast and what actually happens. There may well be last minute changes, such as sick leave which you will need to key into the system. The software then recalculates for the day, perhaps reconfiguring breaks, and lets you know whether or not you can expect to achieve your service levels.

These systems have one neat trick which is determining the best times for you to schedule your training during the year whilst still maintaining service levels.

There are a variety of packages on the market with different levels of sophistication. They start from around $1,500.

You can of course work out all these calculations yourself using Erlang C!

As a quick fix, and to give you a general overview, you can get hold of some basic workforce calculators in the form of a disk, free from workforce management software suppliers. You would input your average call handling time, anticipated call volume, and desired service level and these should automatically calculate the number of agents you need to attain that level.

3g: Multi-media

Multi-media is something of a buzz word and yet it shouldn't be. It is precisely what it says it is - *a variety of ways.* Using multi-media is simply using a variety of ways to service your customers, either via the telephone, the fax, the TV, using video or the internet. Whilst the interaction between agent and customer is still usually face to face or over the telephone, the call centre can utilise multi-media to make those interactions more meaningful and more efficient.

For example, take a mail order company. When a customer calls and wants more information on a particular outfit on a specific page, the agent may have a script to read and have a bulky copy of the catalogue to thumb through if necessary. Alternatively if you use multi-media, the agent could *scan the catalogue on screen*, with the sales script running alongside. Much quicker and easier.

Video

Video can be used to even better effect. Imagine a help desk that receives a call from a customer who has purchased a new laser printer or photocopier and cannot figure out how to change the toner.

The agent can key in the printer or photocopier make and model and ask the system to show a display to change the toner. The agent will then view an actual video of how this is done, with a standard script running alongside. They will be able to describe the process accurately in a mix of scripted language and their own observations. The conversation becomes dynamic and the customer can even work through the process whilst the agent is on the line. Better still, it really doesn't matter whether the agent has had any previous experience with that type of machine.

Emergency services are now using multi-media to help pinpoint locations for breakdown recoveries, power outages and gas or water supply problems. Agents can see a map on screen with the location of the caller and be able to identify exactly where the trouble is. Also the agent's apparent local knowledge creates confidence, vital when callers may be distressed or panicking.

One of the age-old problems in the call centre is preparing agents for marketing campaigns. Where TV advertisements are to be screened, these can now be made available via video to the agents so agents are fully aware of the content and can reinforce the message during call handling.

Case Based Reasoning (CBR)

There is some excellent Case Based Reasoning (CBR) software in the marketplace which integrates video with scripting and search engines.

Basically the agent types in the problem such as 'printer won't work'. The system will respond with a list of questions and the top few reasons why printers don't work. As the agent asks the closed questions and the customer responds, the agent then clicks onto the yes or no button responses. The CBR will then automatically bring up a screen of further questions and eventually reduce the likely reasons down to one and offer a way to resolve the problem. At any stage the system may offer a video display to the agent to help the agent identify the problem, or to demonstrate how to resolve it.

Image processing

Image processing is becoming more and more popular where customer letters, or receipted signatures, are scanned into the system. Should a customer have a query, the agent has access to all the necessary details.

Internet

Recently there has been a great deal of interest in the Internet and questions raised whether or not this relatively new marketing channel is useful, and if so will it replace the call centre and if not how can the call centre evolve to embrace this new technology?

For £10 - £15 per month anyone with a PC and a modem can have an Internet connection and put their own pages up on the worldwide web. There is no difference between the biggest and the smallest companies on the Internet. It is the world wide web which has been the principal driver behind the explosion of interest in the Internet as it provides a standard language encompassing both text and images, still and video. The ease with which links (called hypertext links) can be embedded into any document, taking the reader to any document anywhere in the world is where its power lies. But it is the painfully slow speed of this *immediate* system which is its weakness, sometimes taking minutes just to download one graphic.

However, it is my humble opinion that the 'net will become one of the major sales channels in the not too distant future. For those that agree, an internet strategy for the call centre therefore becomes essential.

The call centre can be integrated with an organisation's web site in any of three ways.

The number of times people visit your site are called accesses. The people visiting your site are frequently called browsers or surfers. I prefer to call them guests.

Email

Guests can send automatic messages to you requesting further information, and this arrives with their own email address. Email becomes simply one more type of message which can be handled by your call centre. Email does not require the immediacy demanded of a telephone call which makes this type of response mechanism ideal for handling during periods of low call volume.

Outbound calls

Alternatively you can capture telephone numbers by asking your guests to register these. You can then initiate an outbound call to see if you can be of further assistance.

Call me buttons

The second method is by using software to offer an on-line application in the form of a 'Call Me' button. This may be somewhat impractical in consumer markets where it is still typical to find Internet guests using a single phone line for both Internet access and normal phone calls. However, in the business market this is a very different kettle of fish.

Already we see applications where the guest can press a button to initiate a call back from the call centre and are given a choice of when - within 5 minutes, half an hour, today, tomorrow etc. The message is put into an appropriate queue for the desired time and this is channelled to an outbound agent accordingly.

Whilst telephone banking is taking the internet seriously, there are enough security concerns to leave many people reluctant to entrust their payment information to a network transaction. This raises a unique opportunity for the call centre to provide a call back facility. However, the Internet is indeed a global village. Your customer could be anywhere in the world and may not necessarily speak the same language or be in an acceptable time zone.

If you are considering a 'call me button' then you really need to offer 24 hour service and evaluate the need for multi-linguists.

CBR on the 'net

One possible solution is to give customers the ability to answer some of their questions themselves. To date, CBR software has largely been used within the call centre itself, to improve the skills of agents and to speed up help desk requests. However, on-line technical help can be offered over the Internet, empowering customers to solve the simpler problems at the time convenient to them.

Users move through a series of pre-defined questions on screen to identify their particular area of interest or problem. They use ordinary English to describe their requirements, and the system will handle misspellings and abbreviations. Solutions to common problems such as blurred characters are shown in both text and graphics. As the software is interactive, they can go over procedures as often as they need.

This cuts down the number of routine queries call centres have to handle freeing up agents to spend more time with customers who have more complex needs and enables the agents to focus more on selling.

This has the added advantage of taking away the tedium and thus enhancing job satisfaction for the agents.

3h: Scripting

Scripting is where text will appear on screen which the agent can either read verbatim or use as a reminder. These scripts can be 'word for word' or they can simply be a bulleted list. There are several software packages you can buy to give you scripting tools and many of the ACD vendors now have either their own package, or a preferred package available.

An example, say with a mail order catalogue, is where a customer calls in to order a pretty pink and green evening dress. The script might remind the agent to mention that there is also a handbag and a pair of shoes in matching pink which would make the outfit look very special indeed. The script might advise of a special offer on a stole or cape in a green to complement the ensemble.

If the customer shows interest but is concerned about the total price, the script might remind the agent to offer extended terms of payment.

Scripts can also be used effectively for outbound calling and marketing campaigns.

Champion & challenger

Where scripts are used, companies usually have a champion script and a challenger script working in tandem. The effectiveness of the champion script is therefore constantly reviewed and changed whenever a challenger shows more promise. As you are using scripted responses, these can be changed virtually dynamically with all agents receiving the new script at the same time.

There are two opposing schools of thought over scripting.

Proponents feel it offers a fool-proof system where agents can feel confident in knowing what they need to say. They cannot forget to upsell or cross sell, or give out the required information. It's all there on the screen for them. They say it empowers the agent to do more and so enriches their job.

It also reduces product training time considerably enabling companies to either decrease costs, or spend more time on training customer service and sales skills. With scripting you can easily multi-skill most of your agents for most services.

In addition you can react quickly to market factors, changing special offers and offering added services just by changing the script. No training or briefing is required.

Some opponents to scripting feel it makes the agents sound wooden and unresponsive. They believe it takes away the spark of spontaneity and the necessity to think, making the job more tedious, more demotivating. Some simply don't think scripting is necessary.

As in many things, perhaps a middle road is the better way. If agents are offered a bulleted list, they are given gentle reminders which helps their confidence but they must actually converse in their own manner of speech and therefore appear more natural.

In this way I think you get the best of both worlds.

Remember though, scripts don't just appear by magic. These have to be written by the company (probably you) and must follow through logically and sensibly.

CHAPTER 4: PROJECT MANAGEMENT

This chapter is for people who have been asked to set up a call centre, or move their centre to a new building, who may not have any previous experience. Perhaps you don't have a Comms Manager or a Facilities Manager to help you - you may be completely on your own.

First we will look at how you select a site for your call centre and the different criteria you will want to consider. Your call centre will need to be designed. You will need to select and configure your ACD and other selected technology.

However, you will first want to develop a schedule, working backwards from the proposed start up date at which point all of the following should be in place:

- Agents and supervisors recruited, trained and ready.
- All mandatory checks and certifications in place.
- Equipment installed, including exchange lines, all tested and operational.
- Air conditioning, lighting and power in place.
- Cabling and wiring completed.
- Workstations installed and operational.
- Carpeting and partitioning completed.
- Design in place.
- Equipment and furniture selected and ordered.
- Building chosen and purchase/lease completed.
- Site selected.

Mark down your target dates and duration of each of the elements. For example, recruitment can take approximately six weeks, and training four weeks so this element must start at least ten weeks before the proposed start up date.

4a: Siting the call centre

Future headaches can be avoided if some thought is given to where to site your call centre. Most companies automatically house their call centre within their current corporate offices and find out too late there are difficulties in recruitment and staff retention, restrictions imposed by legislation or additional overheads that might have been avoided.

How many sites?

Simply put, the larger the call centre, the more efficient it becomes in call handling (see chapter 2 on service levels). However, the larger the call centre, the more difficult it may be to recruit enough appropriately skilled staff. Many factors may influence your decision, including recruitment, cost of properties, cost of telephone calls and management issues. You may prefer not to put all your eggs in one basket (see chapter 5, section on disaster recovery).

In recent years technology has enabled the networking of multi-sites to achieve one virtual call centre giving you the advantage of both more efficiency and the flexibility of several sites. You may want to locate one or all your sites in one or more countries, depending upon your major markets.

In most cases the local development agency, or the commercial attaché should be able to respond to your questions on the following considerations.

RECRUITMENT

This is the most crucial factor. Cost becomes irrelevant if you are unable to recruit or retain appropriately skilled employees.

Language Skills

If you require language skills, the majority of large towns and cities in any country will offer a pool of bi-lingual and multi-lingual individuals. Use demographic information to analyse whether appropriate numbers of people with the correct education, age profile and aptitude are available. A key issue is deciding whether you need native or just fluent speakers.

Competition for staff can be severe if several call centres are located in one town but there is an advantage. You may be able to recruit experienced staff which reduces the start up time. However, they can also leave for other jobs more easily and you may find poaching becomes rife and therefore salaries increase.

Staff attrition rate is often the largest cost that call centres have to bear.

Employee remuneration and benefits

In addition to salaries which differ considerably country to country and region to region, it is items such as the working week, pension, social welfare and holidays that can make a major impact on your decision. Public holidays alone differ widely between countries. The commercial attaché or development agency should be able to advise on cultural differences.

What are the general rates of absenteeism, including reasons such as jury service, maternity (and paternity) leaves? What rights do employees have to time off, such as for studying? Are the work ethics of that country compatible with your objectives?

Unions

In some countries unions possess substantial power and operate work councils as a matter of course. This may impact your ability to react to change, for example moving from a 5 to a 7 day operation may not prove so simple.

Legislation

a) Employee Laws

What are your rights and the rights of the employees? Some countries have stringent legislation making it very difficult and/or very expensive to fire unproductive employees. There may be a minimum wage in operation, minimum remuneration for Sunday or holiday working and night shifts. There may also be legislation for temporary staff and ad hoc contracts.

b) Consumer Protection

If you are wanting to make outbound sales calls, there are very real differences in Consumer Protection laws between countries. These range from severe restrictions including a complete ban on cold calling to no restriction whatsoever. Therefore you may decide to avoid those countries with the toughest laws.

c) Data Protection

There are also differences with Data Protection legislation. You may be required to advise your customers that their details will be recorded and you may not be allowed to communicate compiled lists to a third party unless the prospect has been made aware of this possibility and has not objected.

d) Telephony Protection

Check out possible restrictions on the use of ANI/CLI and how you are allowed to use that information. You will also want to monitor and record calls for quality assurance and to identify training needs. Some countries ban this absolutely. If you want to make outbound calls, or send sales messages via fax, you may find you are breaching the law.

e) Distance Selling

Once a sale has been made over the phone, there may be some countries where this is not legally binding until after a cooling off period, and in some cases a signature is then required.

f) Monitoring

In many countries silent monitoring and recording of calls to control the quality and identify training needs is regarded as crucial to the success of the call centre. In some countries, this type of supervision is against the law. In others you may need permission from an appropriate body, or you may be allowed to perform this supervision subject to using warning tones on the call itself.

The main reason for this type of legislation is the regard for privacy. Not only is the agent being 'listened to', but the caller is also and that can be regarded as invasive. If quality is crucial to your operation, you may wish to avoid those countries where quality control is going to be difficult to perform.

Telephone Tariffs

Before siting your call centre, do a call pattern analysis forecasting the number of calls you are expecting in half hour slices, where these will originate from and how long an average call length will be.

You can then tender out your business by sending this configuration to a number of PTO's (telephone service providers) and requesting quotations. There is no need to look up normal tariffs in any country as you will be able to negotiate rates, particularly if you are planning for high call volumes and toll free numbers. Telephone calls are now a negotiable commodity.

Most countries now offer touch tone phones, ISDN, ACD and IVR facilities but check what penetration of touch tone phones or digitalisation exists.

With deregulation in many countries, don't limit yourself to the local PTO. International companies may be able to offer you a more cost effective service.

Office Selection

Accessibility for staff can make the difference in successful recruitment. Offices that are close to public transport, have sufficient car parking and close to shops are ideal. It is also preferable for the site to be reasonably accessible by rail, air or road from head office.

See also section 4d which covers call centre design and takes you through some of the issues regarding the selection of a building.

Before looking at price tables, talk to the development agencies and see what incentives might be available for a new call centre. Many regions, particularly those with higher unemployment are actively seeking this type of business as it is so staff intensive.

Incentives

There are two different types of incentives available; tax reductions and grants. There are regions that will offer tax free periods to encourage a favourable decision.

Generally, grants fall into three categories:

- capital expenditure, offsetting the initial set up costs.

- salary subsidies.

- training, so that the potential employer is not put off by a lack of skilled staff.

In addition to development agencies, there are also consultancies who specialise in call centre location and will offer independent advice. This can be particularly useful when you are assessing the benefits of a centralised pan European call centre.

Check list

Once you have decided on the number of centres and/or outsourcing options, discuss the following with the local development agency, commercial attaché and the appropriate PTOs.

CHECK LIST

Recruitment:	Legislation:	Office Selection:	Tariffs:
Demographics	Unions	Overall accessibility	Call pattern analysis
Language skills	Employee law	Public transport	Negotiate rates
Salaries	Consumer protection	Tax reductions	Check services
Benefits	Data protection	Grants for:	Select PTT
Working week	Telephony protection	capital expenditure	
Holidays	Distance selling	salaries	
Absenteeism		training	

4b: Tendering

If you do have a choice of network providers in your country, put out a tender for call services. Ignore their standard tariffs and see what each network provider will offer you. Will you be using local numbers, toll free or premium rates?

At this point you are likely to put out a tender for your ACD requirements, including Centrex options and other technologies. As call centres do have a tendency to increase in size, the capacity and expandability of your ACD must be one of the most important issues.

The tendering process is sometimes referred to as the RFP, the request for proposal.

The objectives of tendering are:

- to find the system which meets or exceeds all technical requirements now and has the capacity for growth in the future
- to obtain the best possible price
- to discover innovative ways to meet your business objectives both now and in the future
- what compatibility the ACD has with other systems

An ACD tender is separated into six sections.

1. MIS Reports

As these provide the information which will be used to manage your call centre, their importance cannot be understated.

Ask for the maximum storage capacity in terms of months and find out how the reports are downloaded and deleted from the ACD.

Request samples of all the available reports and find out what degree of customisation is offered.

Also, ask how the reports are created and printed out. Can these be requested ad hoc throughout the day for specific time frames, as well as scheduled to print each 24 hours, each week and each month? Is there a limit on the number of reports the system will schedule and how many printers will it support?

Are the reports easy to understand, or is special training required?

2. Basic Functionality

You will need a list of the ACD features you require, any minimum or maximum capacities and a full explanation of how those features work. Also you will want them to specify upgrade costs for both your future expansion plans and their future releases. Examples are:

- Minimum/maximum number of ports (which will tell you the maximum number of agents and exchange lines available to you)
- Maximum number of ACD groups
- Maximum number of agents per group
- Maximum number of agent groups to which a call can be queued
- Maximum number of printers supported
- Maximum number of RANs (recorded announcements) and maximum length of messages
- Maximum number of call control tables
- Maximum number of steps per call control table

Does the price quoted offer the maximum number in each case, and if not what is the cost to upgrade to the maximum? In addition what other features could they supply you with and at what price?

You will also want to know what the system offers in terms of call handling. How are the calls overflowed, by exceeding time limits or volume or a mix of both?

Can systems be networked? If so, which systems are compatible and how are calls queued and transferred? Is there intelligent queuing at more than one site or are calls diverted blind?

What diversion facilities exist in case of emergency and for night service?

Is voice mail offered? Is any CTI functionality included and if so, what? What additional CTI functionality is available and at what price? Is IVR available? Can calls be recorded and if not, what systems are compatible?

What software packages are available in the price and what can be added? These might include workforce scheduling packages, scripting software and performance management applications. Again, what compatibility issues exist?

3. Supervisor monitor

It is the supervisor screen that assists in the day to day management of the call centre operation and so the information provided is critical, enabling supervisors to make dynamic changes where necessary and highlighting possible problems and issues for action.

Does the screen show real time information or is there a delay? And if so, what is the screen refresh rate? How is the information displayed on screen and can examples be shown? What is the level of customisation?

Will it show individual agent status and queue status dynamically? Will the service level shown be cumulative for the day or in real time? What alarms are available to warn the supervisor that possible problems exist?

4. Basic features

It is important that the basics are right, such as the displays on the agent turrets. The agents should be provided with a system which is easy to operate and helps them do their job, rather than hinder them.

Therefore the way the telephone turret (or display on the PC) is set out needs serious consideration. What options are available and what is the level of customisation? What short cuts are provided for the agent?

Is an LCD (liquid crystal display) offered and if so, what information is made available?

What type of speed dial systems are available and what other functionality exists for the agent? Conferencing? Hot line to the supervisor?

Can more than one headset be plugged in? Double jacking really does offer enormous benefits, yet this is not always available.

What is required to programme analogue sets and digital sets and what is the price differential between the two?

5. Configuration and training

How much systems administration is needed using cryptic codes which means learning a complex language? How much can be dealt with through a PC with easy prompts that only require on the job training?

How much training is required to learn how to configure the system, especially as an ongoing process? How easy is it to place a new supervisor on such a course? What is the lead time? Is training included in the price or is this extra? What is the cost of future training courses for new supervisors?

6. Vendor information

It is important to ensure your vendor will support your call centre through good maintenance and ongoing assistance.

What are hours of support for both the ACD switch and the software application which usually fronts the system? I was once caught out with a maintenance contract for a switch on 4 hour response, 365 days per year, but the PC software crashed on Christmas Eve and we lost all data from that day until 11 January.

What help is available in an emergency, say over a long public holiday? What backup power is offered and is this offered within the price, or as an extra? Are dropback facilities available and do they provide on-line diagnostics?

What is the annual turnover of the company and how many years have they been around, both as a company and in your country? What number of staff do they have in your country and how many of these are dedicated to ACD support?

It is vital that the vendor shows long term commitment to your country and your own ongoing success. What reference sites can they offer that match your requirements? This will not only give you sites to visit but tell you whether the vendor has appreciated and understood your business objectives and operation.

Finally, you might also wish to look at another option of outsourcing part or all of the call centre operation.

4c: Outsourcing

Outsourcing is an emotive subject. In many industries it has come to represent reductions in staff, loss of personal power and loss of control. It has been used by many companies simply to lower headcount, so the very word can cause alarm and anxiety.

However, outsourcing the call centre has a number of benefits.

There are a variety of services available, from outsourcing the entire operation over to a third party, to using an outsource bureau simply as a back up, intraflowing seasonal peak volume or advertising response volume on an ad hoc basis.

Lowering headcount may indeed be a justifiable reason to outsource. Outsourcing certainly takes away the burden of finding an appropriate pool of people to handle calls. This becomes particularly critical if your head office is located in a call centre-rich area and you don't wish to relocate. Then it can become very difficult to find and keep good staff. With employees on a month's notice, high attrition rates and the expense of recruitment and payroll, the headache of keeping your call centre staffed high enough to achieve your desired service levels can become acute. This discomfort can be transferred painlessly to your outsource bureau.

Costs

However, there is another major consideration. Capital intensive technology which is constantly moving forward, requires major financial resources if your organisation wishes to stay at the leading edge. Outsourcing removes this burden, enabling companies to enjoy future proofing technology with no capital outlay.

Direct costs become indirect and if the bureau fails to live up to expectations, you can hire and fire a bureau much easier than if dealing with your own staff and technology. There will always be a risk when someone else is making contact with your customers and handling this key business interface, but it may be no less controllable. The bureau needs to be managed as effectively as your own call centre.

There are a growing number of call centre bureaux offering a variety of services, which can include the entire responsibility of your call centre, handling all your calls on your behalf.

A business case to establish whether a service provider can offer your desired level of service more cost effectively than you can achieve in-house is the first step.

If this is your first call centre or if you already have one which is a non-core activity, has fluctuating peaks and troughs and does not always provide the desired level of service, then seriously consider outsourcing - particularly if you are going to need skill sets that may not be easy to find (languages etc.)

But first, we must assess pricing.

Pricing

It is important to understand what is included in any proposal and be vigilant for hidden overheads. It is essential, when outsourcing a currently in-house performed activity, to fully understand your present cost structure. The same process is required for a greenfield site and projected costs calculated so comparisons can be made.

If you have already calculated the CPC (cost per call) as found in chapter 5d, this will provide you with all the information you need to compare prices.

If not, you will need to work out:

- the fixed costs, including floor space, personnel etc.

- the variable costs such as training

- asset utilisation and depreciation

- the internal costs that will continue after contracting out

- closure and transfer costs if applicable

- projected annual costs

- implementation costs

Having completed your business case, if you have selected the option of outsourcing, you then need to select an outsourcing partner.

You will want to put your business out to tender, and therefore need to document the full specification and the performance levels you demand. Shortlist to three or four companies to complete a full tender document by visiting their site and asking some strategic questions.

Do they currently handle a similar operation to your own and if so could you visit these clients? How important is it to your business if they are also handling one of your competitors? How are staff recruited and trained? Talk to the agents if possible and see if they enjoy their work. Ask them who they are working for. Do they feel they are a 'virtual employee' of the business they are representing?

What is their experience in running campaigns, telephone selling or telemarketing, and how can they help your business flourish?

Ask about their flexibility. If there are market changes which require swift action, can they adapt to your needs? What about their management style and culture? How do they coach and motivate the agents? Can they provide you with detailed reports showing agent productivity and call handling data?

What skills can they offer you? Do they employ multi-linguists, and in what languages. Are their agents mainly graduates and if not, what calibre? How big is the resource pool available to them? What is their attrition rate?

Once you have reduced your list to a manageable number, prepare your tender - the more specific you make it, the less ambiguous it may be.

Include specific questions about the outsourcing bureau:

- **Stability** - ask for their financial information and their track record

- **Quality** - ask for accreditation, references and details of any benchmarking

- **Recruitment & Training** - How do they find good agents, of what calibre and what is their initial and ongoing training, coaching and motivation process?

- **Partnerships** - what relationships do they have with whom, particularly the network provider(s)

- **Disaster Recovery** - what exactly is in place, what can they deliver and within what timescale

- **Call information** - advise your anticipated call volume (details of peaks/troughs with seasonality and trends), average call handling time, the nature of calls (their complexity), what training needs are expected

- **Service provision** - hours of operation, the service level you demand

- **Technology** - advise if there are any specific requirements such as CTI links, multi-media, internet integration, IVR etc. and ask what they can provide for you, such as Post Code look up, scripting, fax back, etc.

- **Fee** - specify how you would prefer to pay - by number of calls, per agent or flat fee for the operation

- **Contingencies** - find out what happens to your calls when all agents are busy. What overflows are provided and where to. Are guarantees given that other clients will not adversely impact your service levels? What are the procedures with (a) fire drills, (b) major powerfails and (c) disaster to the building?

- **Reports** - ask them to provide examples of the reports you will receive

- **Penalties** - determine the processes and the penalties they suggest in the event of under-achievement

After creating the tender document, you then need to develop the evaluation document with a weighted scoring.

List out all the criteria you have charged them to answer and then prioritise the importance of each as a percentage of the whole. Once you have the tenders back, take up all the references and make as many site visits as possible to clients so that you fully understand the role between the outsourced agency and their partners.

Just a word on service levels. These should be guaranteed from the bureau, which should mirror your own company strategy and culture. They should also guarantee that the right number of staff will always be available within the hours of operation. If key people are absent through illness, for example, they will have to be replaced by staff of equal calibre.

However, bear in mind that outsourcing is not a quick fix option. The process of selection and implementation can take up to a year, depending on the complexity of the operation. You also need to be clear about the relationship. Will the bureau be your partner or supplier? How close do you want the relationship to be?

Customers will not be asked for an opinion on whether service is provided in-house or out-house, but they will clearly give you an opinion if the service provided is not good enough by walking with their feet.

4d: Designing the call centre

A major difference between a call centre operation and most other types of businesses is a much higher proportion of employees per square foot.

Parking

When you are seeking premises for your call centre, unless you are building your own, you will find the majority of existing offices may not have enough car parking spaces for the number of staff you anticipate employing. This apparently insignificant item can become a major motivational issue in the future. If people are not able to park their cars close to the office, you may also have security issues with staff working late in the evening or early mornings.

Access

Check also that your building allows you 24 hour access. There are many that don't.

However, coming onto the market are purpose built call centres you can purchase or lease which takes much of the headache away. If there is not one in your area, you will probably need to modify property that has been used for ordinary offices. In this case, if you do not have your own Facilities manager, you will need to hire an architect who will then subcontract the job to a team of contractors. In addition to the general design and partitioning, there is also the electrical wiring and cabling to accommodate.

Facilities

Most existing buildings will require extensive modifications. As mentioned, the call centre is labour intensive and most offices are planned for a much lower density of occupants. This means that in addition to lack of available parking, there may be an inadequate number of toilet facilities. This problem is compounded if you intend to employ more part timers to full timers, as it is likely your ratio of women to men will increase substantially.

First you need a good project programme in order to identify problems. Start with a needs and wish list and then evaluate the practicalities of these against the budget you have available. The project programme should include a description of projected staff levels, business functions, administrative support, computer systems, ancillary spaces, standby power and parking requirements.

Space required

The next task is to decide how many inbound calls you anticipate and therefore the number of staff and the number of lines you will need, today and in five years time.

Again use the tried and tested Erlang C calculations found in chapter 2.

Once you have these numbers, you will then be able to calculate the office space required to house those people. Call centres tend to be open plan and use clusters or pods of workstations. In addition to agent workstations, you will need supervisor desks and a private supervisor office where agents can be monitored, coached and appraised. You may need to have your own in-house training room, if one is not available elsewhere.

Then there is your own office, reception and space for your administrator/secretary, a meeting room, a filing and storage room, a mains room for your ACD and IT equipment and agent facilities. These will include a break room, somewhere for coats and bags including locker facilities and you may also need a 'rest room' where agents can lie down if they are feeling unwell.

Acoustics

One of the single most important elements to consider is acoustics. As all call centre business is conducted over the telephone it is imperative that the agent's voice is presented to the customer in a clear and intelligible way. Background noise from traffic or the sound of the other agents chattering can be distracting and have an adverse impact on productivity and customer service. Try to have an acoustical engineer as part of your design team so that any background noises can be effectively minimised.

Interestingly, the art of acoustics is now so advanced that it can achieve too much 'silence'. If background noise is too low, the lack of sound can subconsciously make the employees nervous and unhappy. In this case, you can introduce what is called 'white noise', a subtle way of bringing the noise level up slightly and therefore making the working environment more comfortable. A level of around 59 DbA works well.

Why not play music in the background? Not too loud so as to be intrusive, but audible for agents. Music can create positivity but again, you won't please everyone so make sure the music is non-offensive to all.

Lighting

Lighting is the next major consideration. Large windows help to make an office look spacious and airy and let's face it, working in a cellar with tiny windows is not a pleasurable experience for anyone. Let people have at least a glimpse of the outside world.

Poorly lit workstations can cause tension and result in eye strain. Some regulations dictate that individuals should be given a personal task light at their desks if they so request.

For overall lighting the most common type is fluorescent tube down-lighting which can work well or be disastrous. The layout of any lighting needs to minimise hot spots of intense illumination, diffusing the light evenly. Distribution of light is basically controlled by the number of the tubes, how you space them out and the design of the diffuser.

The diffuser is the cover of the fixture, usually made up of a pattern of slightly curved reflective material. Select a diffuser which won't attract dust or dirt through static electricity. In addition, as it is the size and depth of the openings in the diffuser that determine the level and direction of lighting, the choice becomes more complex.

Screen glare can be a real problem, causing both eye strain and neck strain as agents move around to see the screen more clearly. This discomfort can lead to increased absenteeism and most certainly to reduced productivity. Soft uplighting can be very effective and prevent much of the glare associated with downlighting.

Still on the subject of lighting, the colour of the bulbs is very important. For example, common fluorescent tubing can be found in around 40 different colours, with some intended to imitate natural lighting. Whichever type of bulb and colour you choose, mark down what these are and where they can be purchased. This will enable exact replacements to be purchased easily and ensure the overall lighting effect is not ruined.

Power

For the call centre to function effectively it needs clean power to be reliably distributed throughout the system, preventing spikes which can crash your systems. There needs to be enough power coming into the building to meet your needs - computer system, telephone system, heating, ventilation, air conditioning etc. You will need to work out the capacity required and discuss this with your local utility provider.

To ensure reliable and evenly distributed power, you may wish to install a UPS (uninterruptable power system) and a standby generator. The UPS will provide power for a short time using batteries, which gives the generator enough time to kick into action.

Take a look at chapter 5, Risk assessment, and consider the cost of an outage on your business.

Workstations

Once the internal layout of the building is designed, one of your first decisions needs to be the type of workstations you will provide for the agents. This decision impacts the electrical wiring and cabling and the carpeting of the call centre.

One thing everyone is agreed on, you should not sit two agents directly opposite each other with no 'barrier' between as it is difficult enough to concentrate on your own conversation without someone else's blasting towards you.

There are two approaches here. One is to sit the agents so

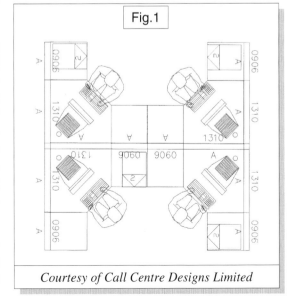

Fig.1

Courtesy of Call Centre Designs Limited

they are sat at an angle to each other (Fig 1) and the second is to put a barrier in-between them to deaden the sound (Fig.2). Ensure the partitioning is sound absorbent to minimise noise levels. However, keep your barriers below eye level so the agents can see each other and don't feel completely cut off.

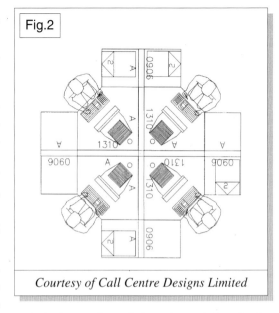

Courtesy of Call Centre Designs Limited

Many countries have laws specifying the minimum amount of space you offer your agents (around their seat) and the size of the desk surface and the leg room offered. Most furniture manufacturers conform to the strictest guidelines but it is worth checking.

Also think about the layout on your workstations for VDUs and telephone turrets. Most people are right handed, but a significant amount are not. Is the equipment flexible enough to allow the agents to move these with ease?

Once a design is selected, the workstations can be mapped out onto the floor area and carpeting, electrical wiring and cabling can be designed around them.

Electrical wiring, cabling & telephone points

Many are the call centres who suddenly find they don't have enough power points or the ones they have are not in the right place. Ensure the drawings for these items are completed after you have selected the workstations and know exactly where they are going to be installed. Many workstations now come with power points and cabling trays as an integral part of the design.

Connections from your computers to the mainframe or server and connections from the agent headset to the ACD all need cabling. These wires need to be attached via an underfloor system or an overhead system. Flood wiring really is essential to protect from leaks either from the roof or air conditioning units.

Ensure your cabling scheme is flexible and safe, tidied away so that it cannot be tripped over accidentally.

Temperature

Consider the temperature. With so many people working in a relatively small area, with computers and lighting throwing out heat, even those countries that would not normally consider air conditioning should do so.

This might be in the form of built-in fans or cooling systems on the actual workstations giving the agents themselves individual control, or a central air conditioning unit.

If the latter, where will the air conditioning units go? If they are housed in ceiling units, be careful they do not blast cold air directly onto an agent below, or leak onto electrical equipment.

Also, select air conditioners that don't just recycle air the whole time. You only need one person with a cold and you'll find that virtually the whole office will be affected. Good ventilation makes for a healthier workforce. It is often poor ventilation that results in problems such as 'sick building syndrome'.

Likewise, check on your heating facilities for the winter months. If you are leasing part of a building you may find there is a centralised heating system over which you have no control. See if there are individual thermostats that you can alter.

You may find agents will open windows making the air conditioning units fight to keep the temperature even, or will switch on air conditioning units that then must compete with the central heating. Sounds a little odd but create a policy for your office as this could prevent some aggravation for you later.

Compliances

You may have regulations to consider and the building may need an official inspection from health and safety officials, possibly including the fire services.

Ensure your fire extinguishers are not only easily accessible but that you have the right appliances in sensible areas. For example, ensure there are extinguishers just outside the mains room and the break room, and that these are suitable for electrical fires. Also train each one of your employees how and when to use extinguishers as part of their induction training. Also give regular refreshers.

No matter how small your offices, ensure there are visible exit signs and route maps showing the location of each type of fire extinguisher and all emergency exits.

Utilising Space

Where are the rest room facilities and the coffee machines? The agents won't want to walk miles to get to these and you certainly won't want that. You may not be able to move the toilets but you can ensure that tea and coffee facilities are close by.

Utilise your space effectively by ensuring work groups are next to each and design the walk ways so that crossing paths is avoided, and people don't have to walk too closely behind agents seated at their desks.

Space is very important to individuals. Don't pack people in as if they were in rabbit hutches. This will not enhance motivation. Instead give people the space they desire. Around 8 square meters per agent is a good calculation.

The Final Touches

Use a colour scheme that is bright and cheerful, and one that people can live with comfortably. You won't please everyone, but you don't want to make people feel ill by using blood curdling reds or psychometric purples!

Pictures & posters

Pictures and posters are important. If the agents are glued to the workstation then it is necessary to have something long distance to focus on from time to time, giving their eyes an important break from the VDU screen. Use whiteboards to show people how well the team is doing, and use motivational type posters or photographs to inspire and reinforce messages.

Plants

Plants help to create a soothing and peaceful environment. Buy some lovely green plants, ones that will thrive in the lighting you have chosen and ones that enjoy warm, dry conditions. Arrange for these to be watered daily as the combination of air conditioning and heat thrown up from the computers makes the air very arid.

Water

Finally, a water fountain in the centre of the office (or more if your call centre is particularly large) really is worthwhile. Talking on the phone all day is thirsty work and a glass of cool water is appreciated, even during the winter months.

Most people work more productively in a pleasant working environment so to get the best out of your most expensive resource, ensure the call centre is designed well and offers an atmosphere in which motivation can thrive.

4e: ACD Configuration

One of your most important and complex jobs during the project is to configure the ACD to your requirements.

As each ACD offers different functionality and uses different jargon, there can be no blue print for how you go about this. Therefore this section will simply address some of the issues you need to consider to make your configuration as effective as possible. The sophistication of your ACD will determine what functionality you have available and may limit your options.

The ACD vendor should provide the initial configuration, but this will be based on your requirements. They also usually supply the systems administration training which will enable you to make modifications whenever you wish, but this is often scheduled after the initial configuration is required. Many systems now offer 'click and point', graphical user interfaces (GUI) which makes the configuration easier, but some still need cryptic codes inputted into a dumb terminal.

With or without training, you will need to advise the vendor how you want your system to be configured and therefore you need to fully understand the ACD and the functionality it provides.

We'll start with routing the exchange lines.

Call routing

We'll deal with inbound first and identify the different exchange line numbers and how you want them processed. Call routing was once a simple question of placing the different call types, identified by their different telephone numbers, into separate queues - if they needed to be handled differently. ACD reports do usually separate out different telephone numbers so you can identify these on the trunk reports, but if you place them all into the same queue, they will all be handled by the same agent group as a first option.

As technology has advanced, call routing has become far more sophisticated. ACDs can now identify numbers dialled and route these (called DNIS - dialled number identification service) to a specific agent or an agent group. If you have CTI, the number called from can be identified and can be configured to be routed appropriately.

So you now need to configure all your exchange lines to route into the appropriate queues.

Queues

Queues are sometimes called patterns or splits.

This is the holding pen for calls and also determines where they will be handled. Once you have configured your exchange lines to route into a specific queue you will also configure those queues to be handled by specific agents or agent groups. You may choose to have skill based routing where the system identifies the call or caller and automatically routes the call to a queue that is handled by an agent group with appropriate skills, such as languages.

You need to map out exactly where you want each of these different call types to be handled, making decisions as to which agent or agent group the call type should first be presented to, and then the interflow to the second and third best options.

The number of queues you have may represent the number of different ways you wish to route calls. For example, you may have two different functions in your call centre that are handled by two different agent types, but your centre is also pan European and has calls from France, Germany and Italy which need to be handled in their own language. You therefore may need six queues.

If your ACD allows agents to be allocated to multiple groups, this works well. However, if your agents can only be placed in one group, you may find you need a substantial number of agent groups with only a few people in each, and a complex system of interflows. Map it out on paper before you tackle this!

Different ACDs have differing levels of sophistication and functionality and of course different reporting mechanisms. If something is particularly important to you, ensure you place this requirement on your ACD tender document.

Interflows

Once you have created your queues, you need to work out your interflows, sometimes called overflows. This is where you programme the system to present calls to a secondary agent group once a call has waited a certain length of time or when there are more than a specific number of calls waiting in that particular queue.

This is where life becomes slightly more complex.

Your ACD may allow a call to queue for two or more agent groups at the same time. However, the system may require you to set an answering priority for interflow calls.

For example, take a call which has been waiting in Queue Alpha. A second call comes in later and is routed first to Queue Beta. Both calls are waiting. The call in Queue Alpha then exceeds the configured parameters and so also queues at Queue Beta. Does it have lower or higher priority over the call already in Queue Beta? Overall it is an older call but as far as Queue Beta is concerned it is the younger call.

One of the dangers is that you end up with calls which are constantly pushed to the back of the queue as new calls come in with higher priority.

Check with your vendor. Sometimes the system automatically prioritises calls and you need to be aware of this. It's also a good idea to specifically request information on priorities concerning internal transfers.

Music & Messaging

When your calls need to wait in queue, you need to decide if you want intercept messages and how sophisticated you want these to be? Much will depend on whether you are offering a toll free number, or if the caller starts paying for the call once intercepted. What type of message needs to be played to which calls, and in what language?

You may be restricted by the number of announcements the system can offer, or the number you have purchased. You will also need both day and night service messages and possibly one emergency type message. In addition, when callers have waited for a set time, you may want to play a new message. How many of these will you want?

Whatever your needs, you may wish to consider professional music and messaging. There are several specialist companies with expertise in this subject that offer both equipment and consultancy.

Also consider the parameters. How long do you want a call to ring out before an intercept message cuts in? Is this delay different or the same for each call type? Once the message has cut in, you may want to play music - what type is suitable? Unless you have your own theme tune with copyright, you may be required by law to purchase a licence with your chosen music.

How long do you want them to listen to music until another message is played? Then how long before the next message is played? How do you want the different call queues to be handled? Which group of agents will best service them? Make a list of each of the skill sets required to handle each type of call, such as specific languages, training levels etc.

Where do you want these calls to go when you are closed?

Tie lines

If you select a stand alone system you may need to specify the number of tie lines required between the ACD and other telephone systems within your organisation, enabling internal call transfers.

Call control tables

With regards to outbound calling, do you want everyone to be able to make outgoing calls to everywhere in the world, or do you want to restrict this? If so, you need to calculate which groups of agents should have access to what dialling codes. For example, you can inhibit all calls beginning with an international code.

Once you have identified all the different restrictions you may want to place on each agent or group of agents, you can create your call control tables.

For example, Table A may have no restrictions whatsoever whilst Table B does not permit any kind of premium rate number. Table C does not permit premium rate numbers, nor international. Table D only allows local calls and emergency type calls. Table E only allows emergency calls to connect.

If you close at night, do you want to password protect all outbound dialling at a specified time so that only selected personnel can make calls outside of normal operational hours?

Agent Groups & Profiles

You will need to give each employee a personal ID number and each ID number will have its own profile.

The profile will ratify the type of employee - agent, team leader, supervisor, manager etc. This determines the functionality available to the individual. In addition it is the ID number which enables identification of individuals on agent reports.

Each ID number belonging to an agent is placed into a supervisor group and an agent group. Some ACDs allow agent IDs to be placed in multiple groups, which can be very helpful.

You will need to attach the appropriate call table to each profile and this dictates the type of outbound call your employee is allowed to make, if any.

Functionality

There are a variety of functions for you to choose, of which most are available as buttons on your telephone keypad. Again every ACD may offer different functionality and a different word to describe it. Here are a few that don't need keys.

Auto wrap up - as soon as a call disconnects the agent is put automatically into wrap up. Not normal practice, but can be useful when the occupancy is too high - this will give the agents an automatic breather between calls. It can usually be set for a specific time.

Barge Protect - disallows monitoring, so very useful on your own telephone!

Call forcing - sometimes called auto answer. Do you want calls to arrive automatically at the agent's headset, or do you want the agent to request calls? Call forcing is normal practice.

The telephone turret/extension/screen keypad

If you select a PC phone, then you will not need to configure actual telephone turrets, but you will still need to select the configuration of the keypad onto each agent screen.

The turret may be allocated to a specific type of employee, for example 'agent' which would then automatically give or inhibit functionality. Depending upon the sophistication of your ACD (or CTI link), each individual turret might be customised.

LCD (*liquid crystal displays*) may be programmed to show information such as the identity of the call - either the queue name, or if its an internal transfer the agent or supervisor name.

You might also display the number of calls in the agent's own queue, or how long the longest call has been waiting. This information is sometimes provided as flashing lights, steady lights etc.

You may want the following keys (note different ACDs may use different names) on your turret:

Activity Code - enables the agent to input a code to categorise each call so that reports can show the number of different types of call received. This can be programmed so that it defaults to the most common call type.

Busy - when depressed prevents further inbound calls and should only be used when unavailable due to all reasons except wrap up (e.g. paid breaks, meetings). Sometimes called walkaway. *NB: Take care, some vendors use this word for Wrap up.*

Emergency - either starts to record the call automatically or bleeps the supervisor that something is wrong.

Fault - agent depresses this key if a call comes in that appears to have a problem, for example the agent cannot hear the caller, or vice versa. A fault report will show the number of 'faults' against each exchange line and identify problem lines.

Hold - enables agents to place the caller on hold whilst searching for information. You may wish to programme the system to play music to callers whilst on hold, and possibly play marketing messages.

Log in/out - agent depresses this button followed by their unique ID code. The system then allocates the right profile, including the queue group and call table.

Mute - when depressed the caller is not able to hear what the agent is saying.

Out - assigns an exchange line for outbound dialling (within the parameters of the Call Table).

Redial - last number re-dial.

Ready - when depressed the system knows the agent is ready and waiting for an inbound call. Sometimes called wait or idle. After each call the system will automatically place the agent in this mode unless you have programmed for auto wrap up.

Speed dial - this could give access to an allocated table of frequently called numbers using a short code, or a personal table that the agents configure themselves.

Supervisor - hot key to the supervisor. (Some hot keys do not allow call transfer.)

Transfer - enables transfer of calls to other extensions or other queues.

Wrap Up - when depressed prevents further inbound calls and should only be used to complete work associated with the last call. Sometimes called Busy or After Call Work.

MIS Reports

Every ACD will offer a set of standard reports and some ACDs now give a degree of customisation. In addition to choosing which reports you want each day, each week and each month, also what reports other people might want and you then need to schedule them for printing. Choose a time when you won't need the printer for anything else, as report printing can keep it busy for some considerable time.

Some items to consider here. If your reports can show service levels, check to see if you can configure in your desired level so you can see at a glance whether you have achieved this each day. If you have chosen to intercept calls with your first message at 20 seconds, ensure the Abandoned Call Report shows calls that abandoned just prior to 20 seconds and those that abandon just afterwards. You can then assess the impact of your intercept message - does it hold your callers or turn them off?

The Screen

Your supervisors will use this to monitor progress throughout the day. First what do you want to show on the main screen?

My recommendations are to show data from midnight:

- Service Level, i.e. from midnight to now, what is the current average service level.

- Total number of Calls offered.

- Total number of Calls handled.

- Total number of Calls abandoned.

- All appropriate groups showing number of calls waiting *now*, and the longest wait.

- All appropriate agents showing their current status of ready, on an inbound call, on an outbound call, in wrap up or unavailable.

Some people like to see pie charts and graphs. I personally prefer to see hard numbers!

Parameters

Most systems show each individual agent status and queue status. You can usually highlight any status that goes over a specific parameter.

For example, if an agent is in wrap up longer than you might expect, their name on screen might turn another colour, or flash slowly. Its objective is to attract the supervisor's attention so the situation can be monitored. At a specific time later, the colour may change again or start flashing quickly, warning the supervisor that the next stage has been reached and they really do need to consider urgent action.

Likewise, if you have calls waiting to be answered longer than your desired 20 seconds, this might change colour or flash. Once attention is drawn, the supervisor can then consider what action, if any, is necessary.

You need to select and configure all the parameters for both agent status and call status.

QUICK GUIDE TO CONFIGURATION CONSIDERATIONS

- *Identify the different exchange lines inbound and group them according to where you wish them to be handled (called queues).*

- *List the skill sets required for each call queue type* and *identify the number of agent groups you need to handle the different call types.*

- *Map out how you want your calls to interflow between agent groups.*

- *Decide how long you want calls to ring out for until they are intercepted by an announcement and calculate the length of time you want callers to wait between messages.*

- *Identify the different messages you require and map these to the exchange lines and choose the music on hold.*

- *Decide where calls should go when the office closes.*

- *If appropriate calculate the number of tie lines required.*

- *Identify any outbound restrictions you want to place by agent or agent group.*

- *Work out call tables to reflect the desired restrictions and permits including password protection for out of hours calling.*

- *Choose the type of agent ID numbering system you want.*

- *Create an employee profile for each employee group, attaching call tables.*

- *Decide how you want each telephone/keypad formatted and with what functionality.*

- *Configure and schedule your daily, weekly and monthly reports. You may need to customise these and schedule them into the system for daily printing.*

- *Decide what information you would like to show on the main supervisor screen.*

- *Determine warning parameters for status of calls and agents.*

4f: Certifications and implementation checks

Different countries will have different legislation so check with your network provider and ACD vendor with regards to the installation of your exchange lines, terminating on the ACD.

You may need to have connection inspections and receive certification for the installation before you are connected to the public network.

Your cabling and electrical wiring standards including the power arrangements throughout your building may also be subject to legal standards. Check with your contractors, and with your local utility companies.

Fire precautions and health and safety checks and certification may be required by the various authorities.

Also check to see whether you need to display any documents or certificates within your call centre. Some countries demand your company registration to be displayed prominently.

Check with your head office to ensure your building and contents are fully covered under an insurance premium.

CHAPTER 5: OPERATIONS

This section covers the operational aspects of call centre management such as health and safety issues, benchmarking and teleworking.

Lumped into this section is calculating the Cost per Call which is a very handy figure to know, particularly when you are looking at the cost benefits of outsourcing. It is also beneficial to know when discussing the value of customer retention and sales and comparing costs each year.

5a: Risk Assessment

A disaster can come in many forms. Most people think of the death and destruction caused by bombs in war zones or from terrorist activity. As incidents of this enormity are rare, many companies simply don't consider disaster recovery plans until it's too late. A disaster can, however, come in many shapes and forms and pose significant problems for the call centre.

You need to figure out what happens to your inbound calls if a JCB suddenly digs up your telephone cables, or your building is destroyed by fire. No matter how unlikely it is that such an incident will occur, it is still sensible to work out what you need to do with your calls each time a fire alarm sounds, either as a practice drill or even in error. It's too late worrying about it while all your agents are standing around in the staff car park for half an hour waiting for the all clear. A hoax bomb threat can result in an evacuation from your premises for several hours while the police make a full investigation.

Unlikely things happen. There were companies left without power for up to two weeks following the once-every-500-years-hurricane in Southern England in 1987. I know, I was one of the last. It took 13 days before my power was restored.

What is happening to your calls?

So whilst your staff are standing outside, or when you have no power, what is happening to your calls? Are they ringing with no answer? Have they received your intercept message and are they being told over and over that an agent will be with them in just a moment? Are your competitors picking up your customers? What contingency plans do you have in place?

But what is the likelihood of anything going wrong? And if it does, what impact is it going to have? You won't know this unless you complete a full risk assessment of your operation and each type of call. After this is completed you can develop a sound, practical disaster recovery programme.

First you need to analyse the business processes looking at the customers actions and agent responses. It is possible to gain an overview by dialling in and documenting each stage of the call. Although this approach will not cover all eventualities the detail is sufficient for the risk assessment process.

Look at each of your services and identify which are time sensitive and which are revenue sensitive so that you know what should be supported first in the event of a disaster.

For example, sales calls made in response to a direct marketing effort, i.e. TV advertising, have a short life cycle before the sales lead is dead and will usually require re-advertisement to generate new sales calls. Therefore this type of call has high time criticality and high cost to recover. However, billing enquiries are clearly less time critical and recovery costs are lower as the only real impact is customer delay in payments due to a late bill.

Identify all the different ways you would be able to maintain your services and ascertain how feasible, easy and costly these would be to achieve. First, develop a matrix of how a call is handled from start to finish.

1. caller has telephoned the correct number and the call is established from their handset to the network provider

2. call is routed over the public network

3. and is routed to the main circuit into the building from network provider

4. arriving at the equipment cabinet (terminating equipment) provided by the network provider

5. then connecting to the ACD (automatic call distributor) which then

6. distributes the call to an agent via a cabling infrastructure which carries the call through the building to the agent

7. who then utilises computer based application to

8. resolve the caller's issue

9. agent satisfies customer request and closes the call, caller hangs up and possibly after which

10. the Back office system deals with the request and completes

the customer requirement

Once this full list is completed, use historical data and brainstorming techniques to identify the risks for each stage. For example, the risks identified against "cabling infrastructure carrying call through the building to the agent" include:-

1.   headset broken

2.   damage to cable from headset to floor outlet

3.   damage to floor outlet

4.   damage to cable from floor outlet to ACD

This analysis produces a long list of identifiable risks where the customer delivery process can break down or fail completely and links it with the technology.

Identify each risk and then analyse it for its probability of occurrence (where documentary evidence is not available, make realistic estimates) and then for its anticipated impact on the customer. The probability of the risk is assessed using the following criteria:-

- High probability   More than 1 failure per month

- Medium probability   More than 1 failure in 9 months

- Low probability   More than 1 failure in 3 years

The impact of the risk on the customer is then assessed using the criteria below. These risks represent immediate impact on the business.

- High Impact   Affects more than 100 customers

- Medium Impact   Affects more than 16 customers

- Low Impact   Affects between 1 and 16 customers

These two assessments are combined using a classifications of risks table to produce an overall risk assessment.

All risks are separated into three categories, Low, Medium and High impact to the business.

You then need to identify two or three options or contingencies for each risk. Each option must be clearly costed detailing the capital and operational expenses. It is suggested that all risks be addressed even if a "do nothing" option is selected.

At least the impact of a problem with each individual process will be clearly understood and a knowledgeable business decision can then be made. The options identified should be incorporated within a staged implementation programme which will include any technology changes, process alterations and people training.

This risk assessment method clearly shows where a risk will impact a customer, how many will be affected and how time critical that is to the business.

This enables a clear evaluation of what is really needed and how it directly supports the business. Spending money on disaster prevention is always difficult to justify and budgets are often not available. The challenge with limited budgets is to duplicate only specific equipment that have been identified as crucial rather than all areas. Therefore understanding where the money should be spent is key to minimising the outlay.

Once all the assessments are made, a disaster recovery plan can be developed by all the key business managers. In particular, it will address *how to* recover in the event of a disaster impacting the business.

5b: Disaster recovery

Due to the increasing sophistication and standardisation of product design, suppliers are continually striving for differentiators in highly competitive markets and one area is fault tolerance. Nearly all IT components are now available with both fault tolerance and duplication.

Your disaster can be placed into one of three categories:

- No building (therefore no call equipment and no agents at that site), example fire - long term problem

- No agents (you still have the building and the call equipment), example fire drill - short term problem

- No call equipment (you still have the building and all the agents), example powerfail - should be short term problem

Let's take a look at some of the options you may want to consider.

Duplication

The trend for multiple smaller call centres is beneficial to disaster recovery planning as the easiest method of risk avoidance is duplication. Unfortunately duplication carries a heavy cost burden. Naturally if you have two call centres, your risk is immediately halved, a disaster in one means you simply divert all your calls to the second. Splitting any risk across three options provides the best trade off between cost and risk reduction but moving to a higher number increases the complexity to the point of increasing the risk of disaster.

However, the downside of this is doubling up on people and equipment that you might not need in one large call centre. Also remember the call centre maxim. Workload is handled more efficiently and each agent is more productive in one larger centre. And, unfortunately, straightforward duplication is not that simple.

If your centres operate autonomously without networking functionality, you will need to divert all your calls across to the second centre. If you lose your building, this diversion can be done from the exchange via your network provider. Otherwise you may be able to programme the diversion with a couple of keystrokes by fooling the system into 'night service' mode.

Exchange lines

If you are considering diversion, you will be limited by the total number of outgoing trunks available as to how many calls can be diverted at any one time.

As far as the caller is concerned, your diversion should be transparent. So if you are restricted with fewer outbound lines than your inbound call volume, your programme should also include busying out lines, or playing a special intercept message. This will prevent callers being answered by the ACD and then left in limbo when the system has no lines available to divert the call.

If you are mainly an inbound centre and use toll free numbers which cannot be used for outbound calls, or you use all your lines for both inbound and outbound, you could find yourself with a major problem. In the latter case, all inbound calls will need another line to divert out, effectively reducing your exchange lines by half. This leaves you with a similar problem where inbound volume will prevent outbound diversion.

Diversion

This diversion method requires a forwarding queue much the same as night service, redirecting calls to another number, because no agents are logged in. In an emergency, such as a fire drill, a couple of keystrokes should place all inbound calls into the one emergency queue, and as no agents are assigned to this queue the system would automatically be fooled into night service. However, instead of routing these calls to a night message, they would be routed to another centre, or bureau. This is ideal when you need to evacuate staff quickly.

Think carefully about how the calls will arrive at the second call centre. Will the recipients be aware it is a diverted call? This takes on particular significance if your second centre is in a different country, speaking a different language. Will your calls be routed to the right linguist?

The recipient call centre needs to be aware as early as possible so that they can action emergency procedures to get more people on the phones. It is likely their call volume is going to double and they may need to evoke contingency procedures to handle the unexpected call volume.

If the recipient call centre is unable to handle such a sharp increase in workload, either because they would not have enough staff available, or they don't have enough workstations, or not enough lines in or ports on the ACD to take the call volume, then this entire contingency plan will fail.

IVR & Voice Mail

If you lose your agents, but have your building, you may be able to send all your calls to voice mail boxes, or perhaps through an IVR system which might handle some of the calls. IVR might be able to divert some calls, handle others and direct the remainder to a voice mail box. These facilities would certainly improve single site resilience.

If all your calls are given just two options to either call back or leave a message, this puts the pressure on when you return. Your call volumes will peak as people ring back yet you also have the additional workload of the call backs you need to make. Would this be manageable? Could another centre pick up some of the call backs for you?

Outsourcing

For short or long term problems, you may find using a bureau is going to be your best bet. Whether you have your building or not, you can divert all your calls through to your bureau. But will they be able to handle your surprise call volume? What kind of response mechanism do they offer? Do they have access to your host database and are their agents trained in your product and services? Or will they be used simply as a live answering service, until you have your own facilities back?

Disaster Recovery Facilities

There are two very different facilities available for call centres, one suiting smaller operations and one ideal for larger centres, both usually requiring payment of insurance type premiums for use of the services, rather than a pay-as-you-go system.

You can insure both your telecommunications equipment and your data equipment with network providers and in the event of a disaster, they will set up a mobile recovery unit outside or close to your offices within x number of hours. This enables you to set up a temporary call centre.

Naturally there is no way you can fit 350 bodies into one mobile van and a huge fleet of vehicles parked on the High Street might just be a little awkward. Therefore this option is not so suitable for major call centres, but ideal for smaller units. Your agents would then operate out of the mobile unit for as long as it takes to get your building back into shape. The network providers detach the telecommunications and data communications cabling from your building and reattach them directly into the mobile unit. Check with your network providers.

Secondly, there are a growing number of bureau that offer emergency facilities for any size call centre. They have premises kitted out as operational call centres and these remain empty until they are required. In the event you lose your building, both the telecommunications and data cabling is rerouted onto their site. Your agents would simply commute to this building instead of their own and work out of it exactly as normal. Many of these bureaux are able to cope with multiple emergencies.

Interestingly, around 90% of invocations are due to computer system failures as opposed to telephony problems and many of these are due to plumbing leaks or leaks as a results of faults in air conditioning systems.

Power Fails

If you have a power fail, do you know how your ACD will respond? Do you have back up battery power, and how long does it last for? Or does your system revert to a normal telephone switch where calls can still be handled, but they are not evenly distributed? The first call will go to the first turret, the second to the second etc. How does your telephone turret respond? Will it automatically ring out or do you need to do something first?

Check with your ACD vendor what is supposed to happen and then purposefully switch off the power to make sure you know what is going to happen.

Emergency Procedures

Create an emergency bullet point list which is easy to follow so that the staff know exactly what to do in an emergency. Place these instructions where everyone knows where to find them - and make sure they are bolted down so they don't walk! These should contain items such as the electricity help line number, where to find the emergency torch, and a step by step guide to anything they may need to do.

In a powerfail, you may want the supervisors to ensure every PC is switched off to protect the equipment from power surges and to prevent the system from tripping when supply returns.

In some cases, once a monitor is turned off, it may not revert back to its 'normal' screen. The instructions might therefore also contain details of how to get the right screen back. It is not safe to assume anything. Switch off your power and see what happens.

Arrange regular "emergency drills" to ensure that in the event of an incident, all the employees know exactly what they need to do. In the event of an emergency, particularly one where there is real danger, the clearer the instructions, the greater the coaching beforehand, the less panic will be experienced. The contingency plans will also be put into action more efficiently and confidently.

5c: Health & Safety

The job of call centre agent is classified as work with display screen equipment, where a PC screen is used for the most part of the day. This type of employment attracts significant legislation in many countries. In those countries where no VDU legislation applies, I do recommend you still undertake to offer good working conditions for your staff in order to ensure their health and safety. A caring employer is an astute one.

Let's first look at some health and safety issues, including RSI - Repetitive Strain Injury.

Repetitive strain injury

A definition of RSI is, " A condition involving the hand, wrist, arm or neck characterised by arm pain and/or discomfort, which has been associated with repetitive movement such as prolonged keyboard use."

Repetitive Strain Injury first surfaced in Australia in the early 1980's and soon developed into an epidemic. In call centres this resulted in increased absenteeism which immediately impacted staffing and service levels. Subsequently RSI appeared in the U.S.A. and then in Europe.

Medical opinion, reinforced by the decision in the British courts (Mughal vs Reuters), is that RSI does not exist as a specific medical condition. Indeed, a study of arm pain in the workplace at Telecom Australia showed an inverse relation between the number of keyboard strokes performed and the incidence of the condition.

Of course this does not prove that pain does not occur in the workplace, simply that there is no conclusive evidence that pain is associated with any particular type of work. However, medical opinion accepts that established conditions such as tenosynovitis and peritendinitis crepitans (disorders of the lower arm when associated with keyboard use) could be caused by repetitive working.

In Australia much emphasis was put on avoiding the use of the term RSI. Alternative terms were suggested such as Occupational Overuse Syndrome. Focusing purely on terminology might appear irrelevant, but it proved useful in helping Australia cope with the problem. Reducing emphasis on the word "injury" contributed to a dramatic decline in the number of complaints.

Despite medical and legal opinion, there is a strong perception that RSI exists and that it is associated with prolonged keyboard use. Therefore it is essential to take this very seriously and to take appropriate action.

However, VDU operators can also suffer with neck and back strain and there are indications that this is also an RSI type condition.

Neck and upper back strain

Independent research by the Institute for Treatment and Prevention of Repetitive Motion Injuries in California confirms that anyone using a telephone handset for a minimum of three hours a day could be susceptible to Repetitive Strain Injury, including occupational neck and upper back muscle strain.

I am still amazed at the number of people working constantly on the telephones and VDU screens that use handsets and not headsets. This means they have to cradle the telephone in their neck whilst they key information onto the screen.

If your call centre is still using ordinary telephone handsets, I cannot emphasise enough that purchasing headsets should be the first item on your budget. In addition to relieving the problem of holding the phone all day, causing back and neck strain, your agents will be so much more productive in a 'hands-free' environment.

Overall, the research showed that headset users experienced 35% less muscle tension than hand held phone users.

Correct seating

The operator chair is also crucial. Sitting in one chair for up to 8 hours a day means that the chair must offer comfort and freedom of movement.

As every person is a different size and shape that means you either need to buy custom made chairs for each employee or you buy chairs that can be adjusted for every individual.

European legislation states:

"Your employee should be able to sit with their feet firmly placed on the floor, the chair seat should not inhibit blood circulation and the seat back should offer firm lumbar support and enable the employee to move freely and comfortably."

To achieve this the chair needs to be height adjustable. Employees who are small in stature may also need a footstool. Chairs should have a curved front edge to prevent the seat from digging into thighs and affecting circulation. The seat back needs to be fully adjustable so that the lumbar support can be moved to exactly the right place to offer the greatest support, regardless of physique. The seat back should also be tiltable to allow the agent to move freely.

However, even if you have the most ergonomically designed chair, it may not help if the agents are not aware of the importance of using it correctly. How often do you sit in an adjustable chair but don't bother changing it? Show the agent how to adjust the mechanisms and if it is possible, let each agent always keep the same chair.

Also explain the importance of sitting in the chair with the right posture to ensure their back, neck and legs are supported correctly.

Many people believe there is a psychosocial aspect to RSI, therefore it is wise to keep stress amongst the workforce at a minimum by providing a pleasant working environment and good people management.

Eye strain

Eye problems can also plague VDU workers. I have already mentioned that lighting is very important. Screen flicker and glare can cause eye strain and discomfort.

Glare on the screen can cause the agents to make uncomfortable head and eye movements as they try to see what's on the screen. Windows may need blinds to prevent the sun from shining directly onto screens. Screen guards can help but use them with care as they can affect the definition of characters on screen and cause even more eye strain.

Neck and eye strain can also be a problem if agents are keying in information from documents. These type of movements can be minimised if you provide a document holder.

Breaks

Adequate breaks away from the VDU should be given which allow the agents to change their focus from short distance on the screen to long distance objects. Many call centres do give official paid breaks morning and afternoon for ten or fifteen minutes.

However if you can offer a different work task that will give your agents a rest from the screen and the keyboard, where they must focus on long distance objects, this is just as good.

There is a school of thought that believes a break of 5 minutes every hour does more good than 10 minutes every couple of hours.

Summary on risk of strain

There are several things you can do to minimise the risk of strain:

- ensure there is adequate space on the desk surface for users to rest their hands and wrists

- to minimise strain on wrists it is helpful to keep the wrist at the same angle as the arm which can be achieved through using wrist rests or placing a soft towel on the desk in front of the keyboard

- offer adequate breaks from prolonged VDU and keyboard use

- get your staff into the habit of using wrist and finger exercises

- in addition to providing the appropriate chairs, inform the operators of the importance of sitting in them correctly

- provide headsets for all agents

- reduce stress by offering a pleasant working environment in which the agents are kept occupied at the right level

- minimise glare on screens by using appropriate lighting and/or window blinds

- provide a document holder

5d: Cost Per Call

Get your calculators out again folks, this is another one of those mathematical calculations that some people love and others really do find very difficult.

To work out the CPC, you need to build in your operating expenditure, most of which will be visible in your annual budget. Your recent invoices should offer accurate costings. Unfortunately this calculation is particularly difficult as it involves extracting sensitive information from other departments. This makes the project particularly strenuous, or should I say challenging?

The benefits

So what are the benefits in tackling such a daunting project? If your call centre operation is sales focused, this information is exceptionally useful. You can work out the revenue earned per call and compare that to the CPC. This enables you to figure out the gross earned profit (or loss!) of your operation.

If yours is a help desk or pure customer service, the benefits may not be so clear. You would need to put a price on the value of customer retention and calculate how many customers your call centre will retain by its existence. This would enable you to use the CPC to show the 'profit' your call centre makes. It becomes very grey, as you may have many customers who choose to purchase your goods and services because of the customer service you provide. This is very difficult to measure without substantial market research.

However, if you are offering a toll free service to customers, then this is where the CPC becomes a crucial element in good call centre management. It can be used to demonstrate the cost effectiveness of increasing your agent headcount. More on this later.

You may also want to compare your CPC with the fees charged by outsourcing agencies, in order to determine any cost benefits.

The CPC is used as an expression of the cost of the call centre and is divided into four sections:

- People

- Technology
- Facilities
- Call Transmissions

To work out the cost per call you have to calculate how much your operation costs for a set period of time, and divide this figure by the call volume handled during that period. So first you need to decide how much data to start with - will one week be sufficiently accurate or should you look at a full month?

If you have substantial seasonal peaks and troughs, your CPC may be more accurate if you use an average call volume. If you do use an average, ensure your payroll costs are averaged too.

People

You will need the following information:

Salaries for every employee in your call centre. This includes you, your supervisors, secretaries, analysts, dedicated trainers etc. If you are working on average call volume during a specific period, use the average salaries during that same period. Factor in the cost of benefits to your employees, such as medical insurance, pension etc.

Also add the cost of any departmental training, which may include travel expenses.

Who else is involved in working for your call centre? What about human resources or the payroll administrator? You need to take their salaries into account and factor in the percentage of time they spend on your business. Also if you have salaried cleaning personnel, resident electricians or telecommunication managers etc.

Technology

This should include all your communications costs such as:

Telephone system (say this cost £250K, and you anticipate a life span of 5 years, then use £50K p.a. for the purposes of this calculation). Include cost of maintenance and any leasing arrangements. Include headsets and telephone handsets.

Figure in the costs of your computer system, PCs, mainframes, servers, printers, software packages, cabling, and maintenance. If you have an in-house IS department, you will need to ask their assistance in providing you with an apportionment of their costs. Basically what does it cost them to service you, the call centre. If they don't know, they should!

Add in the cost of purchasing or leasing faxes, modems and any other piece of kit such as wallboards or electronic displays.

Facilities

If you lease your own building, or lease part of someone else's, you will probably have your square footage costs immediately available. If your call centre is sited within your head office, you will need to find out how much the building square footage costs and then figure out an apportionment to your area by working out your percentage of the space.

Don't forget to apportion your share of toilet facilities, lift maintenance, parking, landscaping etc.

Include here the cost of every piece of furniture you have in your call centre, from your own desk to the agent workstations, and again calculate their life span and divide the total cost by the number of useful years. If your agents have use of other furniture, for example a shared canteen, ask for the cost of the canteen operation (including square footage) and divide it by the number of heads in your organisation that have access to it. Then multiply by the number of people in your call centre.

Figure in all your other operating budget items, such as stationery, utilities, and other capital outlays such as photocopiers, scanners etc. Remember to include any costs for leasing equipment, such as a water cooler, or coffee machine.

Call Transmissions

What do your calls both inbound and outbound, telephone and fax, cost? What about your exchange lines and networks? If you are not offering toll free service, then the simplest way is to take a look at your most recent invoice and divide the costs into the number of calls you received during that same period. This gives you the call transmission cost per call.

If, however, you do offer toll free or local cost numbers to customers, it is extremely useful to work out the cost per call second. By doing this you may be able to show that your operation costs are higher when you are understaffed, have poor service levels with calls holding for long periods - costing substantially more than if you were adequately staffed. An excellent lever you can use to gain hiring authority.

Cost per call second

To work out the cost per call second, first add together the average queue time and talk time (in seconds). Then multiply your specified call volume by this total to get the total number of call seconds. Take your costings and divide this by the total number of call seconds.

How many call seconds would an extra agent shave off your queue time? By increasing the salary cost component and reducing the call transmission cost component, you may find it becomes cost effective to add extra agents.

Next?

Organise your costings so they all have the same time value, say one week. Add them all up together and divide by the number of calls you have handled (not offered), then add in the call transmission price to get the total CPC.

Reducing the cost per call

If you then calculate the percentage costs of people, technology, facilities and call transmissions you can see clearly where the heavy cost burden is - people. You will usually find technology and facilities are the lowest figures, which means it is probably advantageous to focus on people and call transmissions if you need to reduce your call centre budget. Interestingly these are the two variables. Facilities and automation are mainly fixed costs that cannot be reduced. You may find it worthwhile and more cost effective to buy in more technology in order to achieve a reduction in headcount.

But before you start thinking about losing staff, look at what else you can do to reduce the overall costs.

The first major task is to try and improve agent availability without compromising training schedules. Look at your agent shrinkage first and see whether this could be reduced, even fractionally. What is your agent adherence factor like? Could some agent training in the short term improve adherence factor in the longer term?

Can all your agents touch type? If they have to look at the keyboard to find the required characters they may be wasting precious time. Consider a special course to improve agent keyboard skills which can reduce call handling time by as much as 15%. Plan for the future and consider your recruitment specifications. Would it be in your best interests to restrict hiring to people who come to you with good keyboard skills or should this be included in the initial training programme.?

Which agents are struggling with a higher proportion of time talking with the supervisor or taking longer to wrap up calls? What additional training might they need to improve efficiency and productivity.

If shaving time off calls will improve your costings, consider CTI and the value of topping and tailing calls, and screen popping customer information. Also consider the value of IVR and automating the simple, tedious enquiries.

Once you have calculated the CPC, you may find it easier to make a business case for new technology or increasing headcount.

6e: TELEWORKING/telecommuting

This section only gives a flavour of the considerations needed before embarking on a teleworking scheme, and is meant purely to demonstrate that working from home does not simply mean transporting a desk and a PC to an employee's house.

There have been two major experiments which have shown it is effective to operate teleworkers as part of a call centre, with some individuals working from home, and others working from a satellite cluster, sometimes called Telecottaging.

BT Inverness experiment

Much has been written on the now famous BT Inverness experiment which demonstrated that Directory Assistance operators could work successfully at home, given adequate support. The one year experiment involved eleven agents dealing with 750,000 customer enquiries.

BT Laboratories and the Department of Psychology of the University of Aberdeen monitored the experiment extensively and found that:

- Operators themselves benefited from working at home, enjoying the experience and suffering less stress than their call centre based colleagues.

- BT was able to offer a better service to customers, through greater flexibility where employees were more willing to work overtime and swap shifts, skills retention where operators were retained even when they moved to a different part of the country and resilience as bad weather, etc. did not prevent workers from starting their shift on time.

- The Integrated Services Digital Network (ISDN) proved an effective means of providing essential work and support facilities to the teleworkers.

- Videophones are a valuable support tool for remote workers.

Interestingly, the perceived problem of isolation did not materialise.

However, Pacific Bell completed a much larger pilot scheme in the United States between May 1985 and July 1989.

Pacific Bell experiment

In 1984 a request was received from the Olympic Organizing Committee which resulted in Pacific Bell shifting employees from downtown Los Angeles to suburban locations in order to redistribute traffic. After this event Pacific Bell began studying telecommuting as an alternative method of working.

Pacific Bell's definition of a teleworker is similar to that of BT - employees working from a remote site other than their primary business location, who are utilising telecommunications technology as a significant part of their job.

Pilot scheme

They started their pilot scheme in California during May 1985 with 75 home telecommuters and 22 telecommuters working from two satellite offices. This grew to 590 home telecommuters and 25 satellite office participants during the trial.

No special arrangements were made with office based staff to support the telecommuters. All remote workers had access to the same central administration as their office workers. Participants were encouraged to establish a friendship system so they could call with job related questions.

Financial remuneration remained exactly that of their office co-workers and all participants were volunteers.

Project team

A Telecommuting Project Team was created and it implemented the scheme with volunteers as follows:

- Prospective telecommuters and supervisor jointly completed questionnaires to assess the business problems, the quantifiable benefits/results and measurement of the same, and the job responsibilities and physical arrangements required.

- A proposed schedule was then formulated.

- One half-day training was delivered to the remote workers and their respective supervisors.

- Agreements were finalised and signed by all parties.

Pacific Bell carried out several full evaluations, and in January 1988 concluded that telecommuting is a viable management work option that, when appropriately applied, benefits both the company and the individual.

They found that the three primary reasons for people wishing to commute were:

1. to cut travel time or travel inconvenience - 55%

2. to work at their own pace - 27%

3. to save travel costs - 27%

The remote workers noticed significant increases in the following areas:

- output of work increased - 63%

- feelings of satisfaction with work increased - 71%

- feelings of satisfaction with personal life increased - 57%

- the amount of time spent working increased - 70%

The advantages and disadvantages identified by the remote workers were:

- increase in work output - 87%

- working too much - 26%

- having fewer distractions - 75%

- lack of support tools - 32%

- less job related stress - 57%

- reduced social interaction - 28%

- to work on own initiative - 52%

- 85% of remote workers considered themselves successful telecommuters

- 96% of remote workers were satisfied with telecommuting

- 69% of remote workers thought their supervisor had a favourable evaluation with only 6% feeling the opposite.

The results from the supervisors were:

· 28% felt it was more difficult to manage a remote worker than an office worker and expressed concerns with assessing work performance, communication difficulties and maintaining the spirit of teamwork.

· 61% stated that managing remote workers was no different to office workers, and 6% advised it was easier due to the satisfaction felt by the employees.

· 67% noted increased productivity with 57% advising reduced absenteeism.

Manager survey

In July 1989 Pacific Bell conducted a massive survey amongst 6,256 Pacific Bell Managers of which 55% participated.

In short, the survey showed that those managers with experience of remote working are significantly more positive about the beneficial effects on productivity than those without.

· employee stress (87%) and absenteeism (79%) would be reduced

· job satisfaction would be greater (70%)

· employees would put in the same (40%) or greater (40%) hours

· productivity would be greater (64%) or unchanged (30%)

· costs would probably decrease (48%) or stay the same (26%)

· liability risks would be unaffected or decline (76%)

· promotional opportunity would be reduced (43%)

· information security risks would be increased (41%)

· resolving performance problems would be more difficult (54%)

· potentially greater intrusion of family matters (42%)

Conclusion

Pacific Bell's conclusion was that it supports telecommuting as a powerful opportunity for applying Information Age technology and when appropriately applied it benefits the company, the individual and society at large.

Pilot Programme

There are organisations bold enough to go straight into a teleworking programme after seeing the benefits to worker, customer and company. A compromise for those companies experiencing corporate resistance is to start with a pilot trial. Once this is running successfully, it can be added to.

First you must have a sound business reason for introducing teleworking. Teleworking can offer solutions to the following situations and offer additional benefits:

- more office space required, or a reduction in office space desired
- more flexibility required from workers to match call patterns
- difficulty in recruiting resulting in the need to look further field for qualified staff
- desire to retain skilled staff who might otherwise need to resign for family reasons such as moving away, maternity
- if applicable, a need to comply with local commuting reduction regulations
- recruitment opportunities for the disabled
- increased employee satisfaction
- improved customer service

The first steps are the following:

Identify suitable jobs for teleworking

There are 5 characteristics to be evaluated. Teleworking is suited to the following types of work:

1. work that processes information, rather than manual work
2. work with the least physical requirements (e.g. storage, bulky equipment)
3. where output can be defined and performance measured

4. where there are defined work hours so that productivity can be assessed

5. where almost all communication is accomplished over the telephone network

Analyse the costs and the benefits

Costing should include the design of home offices, furniture and equipment including transport to the home and installation costs, legal contracts, additional training for both managers and teleworkers, workshops for the families involved, measuring and monitoring the scheme.

Costs should be calculated per head, for the first year and then the running costs afterwards. Compare these with the costs per head of office bound workers and then correlate this with the added benefits of teleworking.

Plan the technical and work process requirements

Study what is required presently by people doing the job in the office. All the existing information flows and interactions should be noted and no element should be overlooked, including any social aspects. This includes all the equipment required by the operator and the connection to the host systems.

Most ACDs now support teleworking, but by no means all. Check the feasibility of teleworking with your supplier, looking closely at call distribution, monitoring and MIS reports. Check that your teleworker's home is on a digital network as this may dictate the level of functionality available from your ACD.

Consider a video link so that your teleworkers can see their supervisor when conversing, minimising any feelings of isolation.

Design the support system which will include methods of the following:

- Signing in to duties
- selecting annual leave
- sickness reporting
- swapping duties/leave/days off

- training
- overtime payment claims etc.

Select the trial participants

Not everyone will be an ideal home worker and the following personal qualities need to be established:

- Self motivation and discipline
- capability of working with little or no supervision
- safety consciousness
- flexibility
- good organisational and communication skills
- ability to balance work and domestic responsibilities

Trial participants should not be chosen simply because they wish to work from home, however laudable those reasons may be.

Satisfactory Conditions

In addition, the home needs to be satisfactory. Items to consider are:

- digital trunk network availability
- noise levels and nearby disturbances
- security
- statutory health & safety requirements
- availability of suitable storage space
- room to use as an office
- local bylaws
- planning regulations

Also if the potential teleworker is not the owner of the property, the owner would need to be contacted and approval obtained.

Revise the contract of employment

Pay and conditions need to be established and the following agreed:

- cost of extra gas and electricity
- travel expenses when the teleworker is required to attend the office
- taxes which could affect the company or the home worker
- use of business equipment at home
- use of residential premises for business purposes.

A formal document called a 'telework agreement' might supplement the current contract of employment. It would need to state the possibility of terminating this arrangement, any change to employment conditions, use of company equipment for private purposes, insurance, commitment on safety regulations and itemise any expenses that may be reimbursed.

Tackle the legal and regulatory issues

All health & safety legislation should be complied with and joint responsibility is placed on employer and employee. All current regulations must be observed and full training given to the teleworker on how to operate and maintain the equipment.

All other occupants of the house may need to be informed on the potential dangers of the equipment and the teleworker needs to ensure all children and pets are kept at a distance. Existing company methods on reporting accidents and incidents should continue.

Under the health & safety regulations of many countries there is an obligation to supervise the employees. As far as I am aware, no precedence has yet been set on how this might impact the employer's responsibility.

6f: Benchmarking

I won't spend too much time on benchmarking as there are some excellent books devoted to the subject, in particular 'Benchmarking Customer Service' by Glen Peters, but it is worth looking at how benchmarking can specifically benefit the call centre.

Organisations are increasingly using telephone based service to differentiate themselves from others in the marketplace. However, to achieve a genuinely competitive edge an organisation must consistently deliver a level of service that is perceived by their customers to surpass that of others.

Many organisations simply cannot afford to invest more than their competitors on the provision of service. Therefore to compete on the quality of telephone service, a company must continually improve the standard of service provided and at the same time minimise its cost by increasing its efficiency.

In order to gain a market lead, an organisation must be more effective than that of its competitors. In other words, the company must adopt *best practice* within the industry.

Best practice

So how do you achieve this? In reality, most call centres will contain at least one element of innovation that may or may not give them some degree of a lead over their competitors. Leading edge companies however have an ability to combine a number of elements of best practice which together can create a significant advantage.

Best practice can of course be achieved through innovation inside your own organisation. However it is likely that most innovation has already been discovered and implemented elsewhere. So in order to achieve best practice in a call centre, managers might look beyond the walls of their own organisation to see what others are doing.

The process of analysing organisations or products using as similar measures as possible so that apples can be compared with apples is called benchmarking.

However, don't confuse benchmarking with unstructured visits to other organisations or simply copying methods. Benchmarking involves the structured collection and evaluation of data. The accuracy of the project therefore depends on the willingness of target companies to release the information.

Study other organisations

Real advantage is achieved by studying other organisations in three ways:

If managers understand both the strengths and weakness of all of their competitors' services, they can apply a combination of the best practices across the industry to create a service that surpasses any other. If one company boasts a lead through using specific technology and another through particular training techniques, by studying both organisations you may be able to combine these resulting in an overall advantage.

Secondly, because the operation of a call centre is frequently similar between different sectors, it is possible to study and apply practices between non competing organisations. For example, some of the staff contract arrangements now being used by some utility companies could be beneficial to other markets such as Finance and Telecommunications.

Finally, significant leaps in performance and quality can often come as a result of applying a concept or technology that was originally invented for a different purpose. For example the world wide web was originally created for academia and is now being used for commerce.

Having studied practices in other organisations, a manager may decide that those taking place in their own call centres are more effective. The comparison exercise in this case is still valuable as it confirms that the organisation is already using the best practice. It is this reason that many of the world leaders in the provision of customer service are also the most active users of benchmarking techniques.

Naturally benchmarking your competitors is not going to be easy as they are hardly likely to share this information.

A benchmarking process for call centres has been developed by Aspen Consultancy, a TSC Europe company. Their process is called the Aspen World Class Benchmarking Methodology. This is ideal for your call centre and contains three aspects.

1. High Level Benchmarking

Consider performance indicators such as call volumes, number of agents, total call centre costs etc. This analysis can provide effective pointers to areas of the business which require more detailed analysis.

The relationship between the number of customers and the number of customer service agents offers an initial indication of the overall efficiency of the call centre whereas the Cost per Second of a Call is a useful measure for quantifying the impact of process and technology improvements.

The average number of calls handled by an agent in any hour can provide a useful means of comparison of agent productivity and the process efficiency. Other measures which can be compared include unit transaction costs, and the average number of calls required to service a particular enquiry.

2. Technical Benchmarking

Any evaluation for investment in new systems should include an assessment in a live environment. This is a form of benchmarking as the exercise involves the comparison of the existing system against the potential benefits a new one, based on the performance gained in another organisation.

In order to do this effectively, it is important to extract the most appropriate data from the benchmark site so that the benefits can be calculated properly. The vendors will normally nominate a reference site which they feel will demonstrate their product most effectively. This may not be the site which matches your own business.

Whilst there may not be any choice, it is important that you find a reference site that most closely matches the services offered by your own call centre. This means data collected for the benchmarking is more likely to produce realistic calculations for your own business case.

For example, if a company is evaluating the investment in a new ACD system to provide the handling of calls between multiple sites, it is important that the reference organisation has not only multiple site working, but also has the best match in terms of the number of sites, the call volumes and talk times so that a realistic comparison can be made.

3. Performance Benchmarking

Clearly, extracting information from competing organisations is not going to be easy. It is however possible to compare the performance of organisations by emulating customers or prospects and simply calling the organisations and comparing the experiences against those with calls to your own organisation.

Both quantitative data such as talk time and average speed of answer is normally collected, along with qualitative measures such as accuracy of the information provided and the friendliness, helpfulness and professionalism of the agent. Thus both the efficiency of the operations and the perceived level of quality can be compared between the organisations.

Essentially, every process within each organisation is mapped and the results are compared. The objective is to redesign these processes to achieve best practice throughout. The result of this exercise is a fundamental evaluation of the way the call centre functions and therefore such benchmarking is normally undertaken as part of a process re-engineering project.

Best of Breed or World Class

Customers' expectations of service over the telephone are rarely driven by one industry sector alone. If a customer can call to book a ticket on an airline, their perception of the service may be judged against other carriers if they are calling around to compare prices and availability.

On the other hand customers of a telebanking service may have never called any its competitors' numbers because they have always held their account with the same bank. Therefore, their perception of quality from the bank will be judged against that from non competing organisations such as their telephone company or an airline. As a result, all these organisation's standard of service is being judged against both their direct competitors and other industries.

Managers therefore cannot ignore the services provided by non competing organisations. Whilst they are not competitors in goods and services, the general public is comparing these companies and their expectations can result in satisfaction or disappointment.

Customers are also increasingly being exposed to organisations from overseas markets. Therefore if an organisation is to compete to provide service excellence, it is competing on a global stage across all sector. To achieve this, it must deliver World Class Customer Service.

In the Aspen/Coba World Benchmarking grid, a call centre is evaluated in four different contexts :

- the culture of the organisation
- the quality of the service provided
- the technology used
- the efficiency of delivery

Under these headings a call centre is considered under a variety of different categories. The resulting scores are totalled and mapped on to a grid for quality and technology.

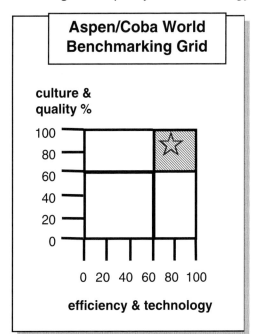

Aspen/Coba World Benchmarking Grid

culture &
quality %

efficiency & technology

The grid depicts the relative scoring of companies' ability to deliver World Class Customer Service. The higher up a company's position on the vertical axis, the greater the quality of service provided.

The further the company is to the right on the grid, the more efficient it is in providing cost effective service.

Only when a company delivers both quality and efficiency can it be seen to be World Class. The organisations which fulfill this criteria are in the top right hand quadrant of the grid.

Benchmarking as a term may be just another piece of management jargon, but the practice of comparing and learning from allies and competitors is not new.

In order to create a culture of continuous improvement and to be the best in the industry, you need to constantly challenge the way you operate, compare your service with others, whilst taking advantage of the best methods and adapting quickly to changes and new ideas.

NORTEL MERIDIAN CALL CENTRE
A BACKGROUND

Introduction

Nortel's Meridian Call Centre is advanced, fully digital, integrated and designed to meet today's exacting Customer Call Centre requirements. Meridian Call Centre will ensure an optimum level of call handling by providing a versatile range of modular software which can be combined with a Meridian 1 digital Private Branch Exchange (PBX) to support a high level management information system, Interactive Voice Response (IVR) and Computer Telephony Integration (CTI).

The number of Meridian Call Centre installations across the world is indicative of its wide acceptance by the call centre industry. To date, there are over 6,000 Meridian centres operating in support of over 250,000 agents, including many of the largest centres in Europe - e.g. Hoseasons, Barclays Bank, National Westminster Bank, Avis, Intel, Hewlett Packard, Microsoft, Interflora and Swissair.

The Meridian Call Centre portfolio follows an integrated design philosophy, consisting of a variety of separate applications developed to work in unison. These modular system applications allow tailored routing scripts to be built up using a range of call control options and voice processing menus to function as either a stand-alone ACD or as a hybrid call centre/PBX.

For customers with call centres on a number of sites, Meridian Call Centres can be networked, thereby offering further flexibility in matching calls to agent resources. The modular character of Meridian 1 Call Centre allows a system to be extended progressively without excessive high cost outlay in the initial stages of installation.

Call Centre Components

The Meridian 1 Call Centre consists of 4 major physical components:

- a telephony system that controls all agent sets, trunks and call routing requirements - the Meridian 1.

- an integrated voice processing system linked directly to the telephony system.

- a management system capable of giving in-depth reports both in standard and custom format.

- an interface for Computer Telephony applications.

These system components combine in a number of variable configurations to meet business needs and provide unique applications.

Sophisticated applications for varying business needs

The Meridian 1 range of telephone switches (Options 11c to 81c) provides a platform for a number of call centre applications supporting from between 10 to 1000+ agents. These applications include Meridian ACD, Meridian MAX, Networked ACD, Meridian Mail, Meridian Link, Networked Administration System, Customer Controlled Routing (CCR) and Interactive Voice Response (IVR).

Meridian ACD (Automatic Call Distribution) - the primary module

- Allows efficient routing of incoming calls to relevant agents.

- Assigns calls to the first available agent.

- Re-directs calls to back-up answering positions.

- Includes Digital Voice Announcer (DVA) delay messages and music feature.

- Plots daily and seasonal traffic patterns so that staffing levels may be matched.

- Displays advance information on subject of call by service/product category.

- Provides real-time information on call centre performance (number of calls in the queue, how long they have been waiting).

- Allows supervisor to contact every agent and intercept/appropriate calls.

Meridian MAX - advanced Call Centre Management tools

- Allows tracking of macro-view (overall system performance) and micro-view (individual agent's performance).

- Provides both real-time statistics displays and historical reporting on the call centre's performance in standard or customised formats on the MAX PC terminal, using high-resolution colour graphics.

- Allows real-time reconfiguration of the system by the supervisor to ensure peak performance: the supervisor's terminal may use passwords to open new agent positions, modify delay announcements, implement night service arrangements and set up automatic schedules to handle predictable fluctuations in call traffic.

Networked ACD - multi-site call routing

- Extends answering capability worldwide and enables call traffic load to be spread across several sites.

- Allows 24-hour personal call handling by redirecting calls to a different time zone where an agent can answer the call, not an answer machine or voice mail.

- Shows network displays and reports covering whole multi-site Call Centre system.

Meridian Mail - integrated voice messaging platform

- Includes voice processing facility to handle routine calls and allow callers to direct themselves to voice mailboxes which automatically dispense commonly-requested information.

- Allows callers outside normal hours to leave details in mailbox.

- Call queue announcements invite waiting callers to leave a message.

- Digital storage allows for high quality audio reproduction.

- Advanced systems features include voice menus, voice forms, distribution lists, delivery to non-user, calling to pagers for remote notification, Call Centre announcements and time of day announcements control.

- Voice mailboxes for agents and extension users provide convenient distribution of internal notices and messages.

- Fax-On-Demand for customers to help themselves to information stored in mail boxes on the Meridian.

Meridian Link

- Enables the integration of the computer and telephony environments, allowing the specific control and routing of a call to be determined according to its accompanying DNIS, CLID (Calling Line Identification) or trunk information.

- CLID integrates call processing with access to customer records by matching a caller's phone number with account data from a PC network and delivering both call and on-screen information to the agent simultaneously.

- Allows call and screen data to be transferred automatically to another agent.

- Prompts telemarketing operators on outbound calls for the following day.

Meridian IVR - agentless call centre operation

- Powerful and flexible applications platform creates and runs tailored IVR capability, allowing callers to receive self-help services.

- Incorporates Graphical User Interface to simplify application development so that non-programmers can build or alter complex IVR applications with speed and ease to accommodate the needs of fast-changing businesses.

- Allows callers to interact directly with information stored in a PC database by steering themselves to the appropriate destination to place an order or retrieve information from a voice mailbox.

- Initiates a defined sequence of verbal prompts, providing instructions to the caller.

- Speech recognition.

- ADSI - Analogue Display Services Interface.

- Internet access.

- No need for additional human intervention, or in a Call Centre Solution used to complement the call traffic using assistance screen transfer.

Adaptability and efficiency

The versatility of Meridian 1 ACD and Call Centre line systems enables an efficient solution to be found regardless of the size of business involved. The popular Meridian 1 PBX system comes in 4 modular sizes (Options 11, 51, 61, 81), thereby allowing selection of an appropriately-sized package. The system also integrates readily with existing telephone networks.

Even though the Meridian 1 ACD system is proprietary and runs only on the Meridian PBX system, if the user has an existing alternative PBX system, a cost-effective solution may be found through the use of an Option 11 as a stand-alone call centre platform.

Future developments

The Meridian Call Centre is designed to be future-proof and new developments and applications are available to existing Meridian 1 users as upgrades. This is part of Nortel's "Evergreen" policy which allows customers to grow their telephone systems in parallel to their growing needs.

NORTEL AT A GLANCE

Company name:	Northern Telecom Limited (Nortel).
Traded:	London, Tokyo, New York, Montreal, Toronto and Vancouver stock exchanges.
1995 Revenues:	US $ 10.7 billion.
1994 Earnings:	US $ 469 million.
Number of employees:	Approximately 63,000 worldwide.
Installed base:	Nortel has sold or has on order the equivalent of more than 110 million ports of fully digital switching systems - more than any other company in the world.
Chief Executive:	Jean C Monty (President and Chief Executive Officer).
Ownership	BCE Inc, a management holding company, owns 52.3 per cent of Nortel Limited, as of December 31, 1994.

NORTEL IN EUROPE, THE MIDDLE EAST, C.I.S. AND AFRICA

1995 Revenues   US $2.6 billion

24 percent of total worldwide revenues as of Dec 31 1995

Employees   Approximately 9,800

Locations:		
Austria	France	Romania
Bahrain	Germany	Saudi Arabia
Belgium	Hungary	South Africa
Bulgaria	Italy	Slovak Republic
Czech Republic	Netherlands	Spain
Commonwealth of Independent States	Norway	Sweden
	Oman	Switzerland
Denmark	Poland	Turkey
Egypt	Portugal	United Arab Emirates
Finland	Republic of Ireland	United Kingdom

HISTORY

Nortel began operating in Europe as a sales function, consolidating its activities throughout the region by creating Northern Telecom plc in 1983, based in the United Kingdom.

Since that time, Nortel has continued its expansion in Europe, the Middle East and Africa and is now represented in the region by two organisations: for the UK, Nortel Limited, headquartered in London, and Nortel Europe, based in Paris.

The company's growth in the region has been achieved by working closely with a network of independent distributors and licensees.

Key developments include:

- the acquisition of STC plc in 1991
- the joint venture in France with Lagardère Groupe in 1992 (Matra Communication and Nortel Matra Cellular)
- the joint venture in Germany with Daimler-Benz Aerospace AG in 1995 (Nortel Dasa Network Systems)
- the joint venture in Italy with Olivetti SpA in 1995 (Sixtel)
- the controlling interests in Turkey in Netas - Northern Electric Telekomunikasyon A.S.
- the opening of an office in Moscow in 1995, as a base for the rapidly-growing business in the Commonwealth of Independent States (CIS).

BUSINESS ACTIVITIES AND ACHIEVEMENTS

For the past three years, Nortel has been marketing its complete product portfolio to major customers in the region, both directly and via an accredited group of telecommunications distributors and service.

Wireless networks

Nortel has won contracts in:

Israel - with CellCom Israel Ltd to supply Israel's second nationwide cellular mobile telephone network under a three-year, US$100 million agreement.

CIS - with Uzdunrobita to extend digital cellular coverage to the top five cities of Uzbekistan, a republic in the CIS.

France - Nortel's US$100 million supply agreement for personal communications network (PCN) radio infrastructure to Bouygues Telecom has recently been incremented by US$50 million for the expansion of its network to the Côte D'Azur and Lyons regions, and for further coverage in the Ile de France area.

France - Nortel has equipped over half the territory covered by France Telecom's Itinéris GSM network, including the entire South of France in 1992-3, and Normandy, Charentes and Centre of France in 1994. In 1995, Nortel was involved in the rapid deployment of the Itinéris network, helping France Telecom double their capacity in less than one year.

Austria - In December 1993, the Austrian public network operator chose Nortel's cellular switching systems for its GSM network.

Tunisia - A contract was signed in May 1994 with the public network operator for a complete GSM network covering metropolitan Tunis.

Belgium - Nortel has won a US$33 million contract for the supply of radio infrastructure equipment for Mobistar, the second licensed operator on GSM (Global System for Mobile Communications)

UK - Ionica, the third licensed national public telephone operator in the United Kingdom, ordered US$10 million in fixed radio access network equipment from Nortel, for its new commercial service.

Czech Republic - Cable Plus, the Czech Republic's newly licensed telecommunications operator, ordered Nortel's PROXIMITY 1 Fixed Radio Access (FRA) equipment for a trial planned to start in the Liberec region.

Ireland - Esat Digifone, recently awarded the second national licence to operate a mobile telephone service in Ireland, has chosen Nortel to provide a complete system for its new GSM 900 MHz network.

Public Carrier Networks

Nortel has achieved successes with its Synchronous Digital Hierarchy (SDH) transmission equipment over the past year by winning several contracts including a US$31 million contract from Yorkshire Cable, orders worth US$38 million from the Bell Cablemedia Group and a US$40 million contract to supply the Dutch Armed Forces with equipment to develop the NAFIN project (Netherlands Armed Forces Integrated Network).

In August 1995, Nortel was awarded a three-year, multi-million dollar development and supply contract from Concert, the BT and MCI global joint venture company. Nortel is supplying Concert with its Meridian and DMS-250 digital switching systems together with an integrated Network Management capability.

During the latter part of 1995, substantial contracts were awarded to Nortel in the United Kingdom.

Energis selected Nortel as its preferred supplier to provide Intelligent Network (IN) products, incorporating ServiceBuilder™ together with additional DMS-100 switches, to run BCM's pilot data service in its UK south region.

In addition, Nortel confirmed its position as a leading supplier of telecommunications equipment to the UK CATV market and with the installation by TeleWest's subsidiary company, United Artists Avon, of the one millionth line of Nortel's Digital Multiplex System (DMS) switch.

Enterprise Networks

Following a significant 26.9 percent growth in PBX sales during 1995, Nortel delivered its one millionth line of Meridian 1 PBX in the Europe/Middle East region for that year.

Nortel digital networking solutions have been chosen to bring voice mail and other services to guests at Intercontinental Hotels and Resorts in 59 countries.

Advanced call centre technology is powering customer responsiveness at Dell Computers, Gateway 2000, Creative Labs and Best Western International, all based in Ireland, at Ellos, Scandinavia's largest mail order firm, and at Microsoft centres across Europe.

In the Middle East, the Abu Dhabi Police have a new Meridian 1 network while the Ministry of Finance in Kuwait has bought the first Meridian 1 Option 81C PBX (Private Branch Exchange) system in the region.

During 1995, Nortel won a US$4 million order to supply Meridian systems to Russia's giant Lada car corporation, with 3 of Nortel's latest Meridian 1 Option 81C PBX systems and SDH fibre transmission systems linking two sites and serving 15,000 extensions on the huge 60 square kilometre site.

Nortel's wireless office system, Companion, continues its impressive growth, with the sale of the 7000th system worldwide to German aluminium sheet manufacturer Vereingte Aluminium Werke (VAW).

Spain's largest savings bank `la Caixa', deployed Nortel's Magellan Passport switch as the backbone of its Integrated Services Broadband Network (ISBN). Other achievements include the Magellan Passport enterprise network switch as the platform to launch voice over asynchronous transfer mode (ATM) off the drawing board and into reality. The basis of the industry's first voice over ATM network and the only switch to offer variable bit rate (VBR) service for voice traffic, the Magellan Passport has proved that voice over ATM not only is technically viable and reliable, but also economically sound.

RESEARCH AND DEVELOPMENT

In 1971, Northern Electric and Bell Canada formed Bell-Northern Research Ltd. (BNR) as a joint subsidiary to carry out telecommunications R&D. Now Nortel Technology, the research laboratories, is a world leader in the design and development of advanced telecommunications systems and operate or support facilities in seven countries. In Europe, Nortel operates laboratories located in Harlow, Maidenhead, New Southgate and Monkstown in the UK.

In addition, Nortel supports a joint venture in Friedrichshafen, Germany, for the development activities of Nortel Dasa Network Systems. All are part of a global integrated community of researchers dedicated to developing the most innovative communications products and services for marketing and sales by Nortel or its global network of strategic alliances and licensees around the world.

MANUFACTURING

Manufacturing is carried out at the following plants in the United Kingdom and Europe:

Location	Equipment Manufactured
Monkstown, N.Ireland	ETSI standard transmission equipment/ DMS products
Cwmcarn, Wales	Telephone sets and terminals
Newport, Wales	Secure communications systems
Paignton, England	Opto-electronics and radio infrastructure gear
Galway, Eire	Meridian 1 family of business communication systems
Istanbul, Turkey	Public switching equipment

CHAPTER 7: GLOSSARY

Abandoned call | Where a caller has hung up before an agent has been free to answer the call. Also called lost call.

ACD:
Automatic Call
Distributor | A telephone system handling large call volumes which automatically offers the next call to the agent waiting for the longest period. Nowadays these switches are very sophisticated and you can configure them with a variety of parameters in order to give priorities to different callers and send certain types of calls to specific groups or individuals. ACDs also provide a wealth of reports on calls, agents and trunks.

Adherence factor | The closeness and punctuality with which agents adhere to their schedules for breaks, lunches etc.

Adjunct Processor | A name sometimes given to 'soft' ACDs or PC based ACDs.

Agent ID | The individual code used by agents to log into the ACD system. This ID enables the system to track their performance.

Agent Group | In order for the ACD to route calls appropriately, agents are placed into agent groups. These determine which type or types of call they will be offered.

AHT: Average
Handling Time | The average time spent per call and any work required following the call. It equates to the sum of Talk Time and Wrap Up Time averaged out.

Algorithms | A mathematical formula for a computer operation.

All trunks busy:
ATB | When all telephone lines in any group are occupied during which time all further callers receive a busy tone.

Annual trend | The percentage increase or decrease in calls over a twelve month period.

Answer Detect | Where the telephone system automatically makes outbound calls and on answer identifies network tones such as ringing, engaged, unobtainable, faxphones and answerphones and filters these out, only sending live calls through to an agent.

API:
Application
Programme
Interface | This is the translator which enables a telephone system and a computer or computer system to talk with each other and give each other commands.

Application | Software that carries out a specific task, such as word processing or spreadsheets.

ASA: Average speed of answer	The average length of time calls have spent in the Queue waiting for an agent.
ATB: All trunks busy	When all telephone lines are occupied and other callers receive an engaged or busy tone.
ATT: Average Talk Time	The average length of time an agent speaks with a caller, from answering the call to hanging up.
Audiotex	An automatic voice response service where a caller dials a number and receives a recorded message. This can be anything from weather reports and horoscopes to adult entertainment.
Auto attendant	Where an inbound call is answered by a recording which asks the customer to either press buttons on the keypad or say which extension they want. The system then automatically routes their call.
Automatic Call Distributor: ACD	A telephone system handling large call volumes which automatically offers the next call to the agent waiting for the longest period. Nowadays these switches are very sophisticated and you can configure them with a variety of parameters in order to give priorities to different callers and send certain types of calls to specific groups or individuals. ACDs also provide a wealth of reports on calls, agents and trunks.
Automatic number identification: ANI	Sometimes called CLI - Calling Line Identity. A feature which enables the caller's own telephone number to be forwarded at the same time as their call, enabling identification.
Available	Agent status when the agent is logged into the ACD and is ready and waiting for an inbound call. Also called Idle or Ready.
Back busy	Where you purposefully busy out lines during peak traffic so that some callers receive an engaged signal rather than holding for an unacceptable length of time.
Blending	Where a call centre uses agents for both inbound and outbound calling, making outbound calls during troughs in inbound traffic.
Caller tolerance	This may be described as high or low, depending upon the length of time callers are prepared to wait in queue for an available agent.
Calling Line Identification: CLID	The caller's own telephone number when forwarded at the same time as their call,

Calling Line Identifier: CLI	Sometimes called ANI - automatic number identification. A feature which enables the caller's own telephone number to be forwarded at the same time as their call, enabling identification.
Callpath	An application programme interface from IBM.
Call routing	The flow of calls from the ACD as set by predetermined parameters in the configuration.
Call seconds: CCS	Calculated in sums of 100, centum call seconds are the number of seconds exchange lines are occupied. 36 centum call seconds (3,600) equate to one hour.
Case based reasoning: CBR	A software programme which enables problems to be identified by working through scripts of questions and answers. The system eventually diagnoses the most likely cause of the problem and its solution.
Centrex (central exchange)	Generic term for a service offered by network providers (each provider uses a different brand name) which in the context of call centres enables organisations to use the provider's ACD facilities at the exchange.
Computer telephony integration: CTI	Where the computer and the telephone are given the ability to speak with each other and give each other commands.
Cost per Call: CPC	This is calculated by dividing the number of calls handled into the full cost of the entire call centre operation.
Daily index factor	A weight given to each day of the week so that monthly call forecasts can be allocated accurately to each day.
DDI: Direct Dial Inward	Where you can dial directly into a company and reach an extension without going through a switchboard operator. Sometimes called DID.
Delay Announcements	Recorded messages given to callers whilst in queue.
DID: Direct Inward Dial	Where you can dial directly into a company and reach an extension without going through a switchboard operator. Sometimes called DDI.
DNIS: Dialled number identification Service.	This facility enables the ACD to identify the number dialled and therefore route or prioritise the call according to whatever parameters have been predetermined.

Double Jacking	Where two people are connected at the same telephone terminal/turret and can both participate in the same call. Used extensively in training to 'shadow' a new agent.
Erlang	Created by A K Erlang, a Danish engineer, and is a measurement of telephone traffic with one erlang equating to one fully occupied call hour (36 centum call seconds (3,600 seconds) equate to one hour.
Erlang C	A formula created by A K Erlang which takes random call arrival into account and is used to calculate the number of agents required to handle a specific number of calls within a specified time frame.
Exchange lines	Another name for telephone lines.
FTE: Full time equivalents	The number of agents required expressed in terms of total man-hours required divided by the number of hours a full time agent would normally work. This figure facilitates salary budgets and hiring approvals.
Gate	A group of agents handling the same type or types of call.
Half-hour segment index factor	A weight given to each half hour of the day so that daily call forecasts can be allocated accurately to each half hour segment.
Hunt Group	Used with ordinary PBX systems to distribute calls. There are two systems, the first where calls are distributed in the same order each time so that the first extension will always receive the next call unless busy when it will hunt to the second extension. The second system is called Round Robin where the next call will automatically hunt to the second extension, and the third call will hunt to the third extension, etc. offering a more even distribution of calls.
Hybrid ACDs	Telephone systems that can operate as both automatic call distributors and PBXs.
Hypertext link	Used in the world wide web to create a link to another page (anywhere in the world) which enables people to view these by a simple double click of the mouse.
Idle	A name given to agents who are logged in to the ACD and are available and waiting for a call to come in. Also called Available or Ready.
Inbound	All calls received by the call centre.
Integrated Services Digital Network: ISDN	All digital network, which may carry both voice and data and usually leased in bundles of 30 trunks.

Interactive voice response: IVR	Where an inbound call is answered by a recording which asks the customer to interact by speaking or pressing buttons on the keypad in response to a menu of options. This response instructs the system to search for specific information in the host database which is then converted into the spoken word by voice synthesis.
Interflow	After a call has waited for a pre-defined time at its primary queue (or a pre-defined call volume has been exceeded), it is then interflowed to a secondary queue. Sometimes called overflow.
Intraflow	When calls are flowed out of the ACD to another answering point.
Line utilisation	An ACD report showing each exchange line and its occupancy during the requested period of the report.
Management Information Services: MIS	Reports from the ACD showing data on agents and agent groups, inbound and outbound calls, and exchange lines.
Mean monthly trend	The percentage increase or decrease in call volume over a one month period.
Messaging & Music on Hold	Where calls in the queuing process are played messages and music in order to tempt callers into holding longer, and also when callers are placed on hold during the handling of their call.
Night service	Used when the call centre is closed, this might be a message given to callers, a diversion to another centre or to voice mail boxes.
Occupancy	The percentage of time an individual agent, or all agents (average) are actively occupied during talk time and wrap up time. Occupancy does not include ready time.
Outbound	All calls that are made by the call centre.
Overflow	After a call has waited for a predefined time at its primary queue (or a predefined call volume has been exceeded), it is then interflowed to a secondary queue. Sometimes called intraflow.
Pattern	Another name for queue or split. A holding pen for calls.
PBX (also PABX): Privated automated branch exchange	A generic term for a switch, a telephone system, that is found inside a company's premises (as opposed to an exchange belonging to a network provider which serves the general public).

PC based Acds	Software programme which enables automatic call distribution. Also called Adjunct Processors and Soft ACDs
Performance Related Pay: PRP	Part of an employee's salary which is based upon their performance and is therefore not guaranteed unless targets such as adherence factors, quality etc. are met.
Pooling principal	This dictates that the larger the call centre, the more efficient each agent becomes in terms of occupancy.
POTS	Plain old telephone services. A single line telephone service with no frills. You can simply make or receive one call at a time.
Power dialling	Is sometimes used as a generic term for all diallers but this can cause confusion. Power dialling is specifically where the telephone system dials as many calls as it has lines available and, using answer detect, puts through live calls to agents. If no agent is available when a call is answered, it will simply drop the call and as this causes a 'nuisance call' it is therefore not highly regarded .
Predictive dialling	Similar to power dialling but more sophisticated. This uses a pacing algorithm which regulates the number of outbound calls made based on the probability of an agent being available. Minimises the number of nuisance calls.
Preview dialling	Uses screens of data downloaded from a central database. The agent then initiates the call usually by using a pre-programmed button on the keyboard, or screen.
Progressive dialling	The most sophisticated of all the diallers, this goes one stage further than predictive dialling and actually monitors the status of operators before calls are made. It keeps agents supplied with live calls and virtually eliminates nuisance calls.
PRP: Performance related pay	Part of an employee's salary which is based upon their performance and is therefore not guaranteed unless targets such as adherence factors, quality etc. are met.
Protocol	The language used by a software programme.
PTO	Public Telephone Operator. Also called network provider.
Queue	The 'holding pen' for calls whilst waiting for an agent to become free. Also called splits and patterns.

Queue Time	The number of seconds a call waits in queue before handling.
RAN	Recorded announcement.
Ready	A name given to agents logged in to the ACD who are available and waiting for a call to come in. Sometimes called Idle or Available.
Ring Time	The time from dialling to being answered either by a live agent or the ACD Delay announcement.
Rostered staff factor	Erlang C calculations demonstrate how many agents are needed to be available to take calls. After taking into account absenteeism including breaks, lunches and average sickness, you will schedule more agents to cover this shortfall . For example, if you require 25% more staff your Rostered staff factor will be 1.25.
Seasonality variation	The variation in call volume due specifically to seasons during the year.
Screen dialling	Where you select a number on the screen using a mouse to point and click and the system will dial out for you.
Screen popping	Where integration between the computer and the telephone (CTI) enables the system to attempt identification of each call and look into the database for a match. If that match exists, the data attached to it will then be displayed on the agent screen just prior to the call arriving at the agent's ear.
Service agency	A bureau which will handle your call centre requirements either the complete operation or as an intraflow facility.
Short Calls	As defined by you, you would set the desired parameter in the ACD.
Shrinkage	The percentage of time when scheduled agents are unavailable to take calls, such as breaks, lunches and training.
Soft ACD	Software programme which enables automatic call distribution. Also called Adjunct Processor and Soft ACD.
Speed of answer	The time from a call arriving at the ACD to being answered by an agent.
Split	The 'holding pen' for calls whilst waiting for an agent to become free. Also called queues and patterns.

Stand Alone ACD	A telephone system designed specifically for automatic call distribution. Historically these have not provided PBX or autodialling functionalities but this may change.
Switch	The simplest explanation, and in the context of a call centre, is the generic name for all telephone systems
Talk time	As it implies, the time in seconds an agent is talking, from answering a call to the caller hanging up.
Telecommuting	American term for teleworking where people work from home either full time or as part of their working week.
Telecottaging	Where a small group of people work in a satellite office.
Teleworking	The UK version for people working from home either full time or as part of their working week.
Tie line	A private line between the ACD and PBX enabling call transfers.
Trunks	Exchange lines, or telephone lines.
Turret	The telephone console used by the agents.
Unavailable	Agent status when logged in to the ACD but not available to take calls, for example during paid breaks or whilst in coaching sessions.
Voice Mail	Enables callers to leave a message much like an answerphone but this message can then be reviewed, copied, stored, annotated and forwarded to one or many people in one go. Sometimes called voice messaging.
Voice processing	A generic term for a variety of applications such as IVR, Voice mail and auto attendants.
Voice response unit: VRU	A facility which enables IVR (interactive voice response).
Workload	Workload normally refers to call volume. Usually expressed in hours, one hour of workload is one erlang or 36 CCS (centum call seconds) where all trunks are fully occupied.
Wrap Up	The time spent completing work associated with a call, after the caller has hung up.

SELECTED READING MATERIAL

'**Benchmarking Customer Service**' by Glen Peters (UK) *Published by Pitmans*

'**Building a World Class Inbound Call Center**' by William Durr (USA). *Published by Teleprofessional*

Call Centre focus - magazine (UK) *Published by CALLcraft*

Call Center Magazine - magazine (USA) *Published by Telecom Library Inc.*

Call Center Magazine - magazine (Netherlands) *Published by Giga*

'**Coaching for Improved Work Performance**' by Ferdinand F Fournies (USA) *Published by Liberty Hall Press, an imprint of McGraw-Hill Inc.*

'**Computer Telephone Integration**' by Rob Walters (UK) *Published by Artech House*

'**Computer Telephony Integration, the business opportunity**' by Simon Glassman, Paul Lee and Eirwen Nichols (UK) *Published by Ovum Limited*

'**Inbound Call Centers: Design, Implementation and Management**' by Robert A Gable (USA) *Published by Artech House*

Service Level Newsletter (USA) *Published by Incoming Calls Management Institute*

'**Telecommuting**' by Osman Eldib and Daniel Minoli (USA) *Published by Artech House*

Teleprofessional & Teleprofessional International - magazines (USA) *Published by Teleprofessional*

'**Teleworking Explained**' by Mike Gray, Noel Hodson and Gil Gordon (UK) *Published by John Wiley & Sons*

Teleworking information pack from **The BT Inverness Experience** (UK) - call free in the UK 0800 800 854.

CALL CENTRE INTERNET SITES

http://www.callcentre.co.uk/telebusiness
Telebusiness now! - (UK) *managed by CALLcraft*

http:www.telemkt.com
Telem@rket - (USA) *managed by Cyber Marketing Services & Teleprofessional*

INDEX

Abandoned calls, *36, 62, 63-64*
ACD, *35, 51, 69-80, 83, 107-110,
124-133*
   adjunct processors, *71, 75*
   centrex, *71, 75-80*
   configuration, *110, 124-132*
   evolution, *70-71*
   hybrids, *75*
   parameters, *131*
   pc based, *71-75*
   priorities, *72*
   programming, *71*
   reports, *57-68*
   soft, *71-75*
   stand alones, *71, 75*
   tendering, *107-110*
   vendors, *110*
Acoustics, *117-118, 120*
Activity codes, *74, 129*
Adherence factor, *52, 152*
Adjunct Processor, *71, 75*
After call work, *37*
Agent
   availability, *22-23, 52, 60*
   breaks, *147*
   competitions, *28-31*
   development, *19-23*
   discipline, *32-33*
   empowerment, *21-22, 99*
   ID, *58, 128*
   groups, *128*
   recruitment, *10-18, 102-104*
   remuneration, *26-28, 103*
   reports, *57, 58-61*
   scheduling, *20, 47-53, 90*
   training, *19-24*
Algorithms, *82*
All trunks busy:ATB, *54*
Annual trend, *39*
Answer Detect, *82*
Application
   programme Interface API, *85-86*
ATB: All trunks busy, *54*
Audiotex, *93*
Auto answering, *73*

Auto attendant, *92*
Automatic Call Distributor *see ACD*
Average
   handling time, *36*
   queue time, *36*
   ring time, *36*
   speed of answer, *36, 55,*
   talk time, *36, 59*
   trunk holding time, *36*
   wait, *59*
   wrap up time, *36, 59, 73, 128, 130*
Back busy, *56, 140*
Benchmarking, *161-166*
Blending, *82-83*
Breaks, *147*
BT Inverness experiment, *153*
Busy, *129*
   back, *55-56, 140*
Cabling, *120*
Call
   abandoned, *36, 62, 63, 64*
   blending, *82-83*
   control tables, *127*
   data, *61-64*
   forcing, *128*
   forecasting, *38-46*
   handling, *36, 62,*
   me buttons, *97-98*
   offered, *62*
   processing, *35-37*
   reports, *61-64*
   routing, *124-125*
   seconds:CCS, *55*
   short calls, *60*
   transmissions, *150-151*
Caller tolerance, *35*
Calling Line Identity: CLI, *88*
Callpath, *87*
Case based reasoning: CBR, *96, 98*
Centrex (central exchange), *71, 75-76,
79-80*
Certification, *133*
Champion & challenger, *99*
Computer telephony integration:CTI, *75,
79, 85-89*

Configuration, *110, 124-132*
Cost per Call: CPC, *112, 148-152, 163*
Database integration, *83-84*
Delay Announcements, *36, 72-73*
Design, *116-123*
Desktop CTI, *86, 89*
DNIS: Dialled number Identification
    Service, *124*
Dialling, *81-84, 89*
    manual, *81*
    power, *81*
    predictive, 79, *82, 89*
    preview, *81, 89*
    progressive, *82*
    screen, *81*
Direct Inward Dial: DID or DDI, *79*
Disaster recovery, *139-143*
Diversion, *139, 140-141*
Double Jacking, *17, 20, 109*
Duplication, *139-140*
Electrical wiring, *120*
Email, *97*
Emergency procedures, *143*
Erlang, *37,47*
    calculators, *47*
    Erlangs, *55*
    Erlang B, *55*
    Erlang C , *37, 94, 117*
Exchange lines, *54-56, 140*
Eye strain, *146*
Facilities, *78, 116-117, 105, 150*
First party CTI, *86, 89*
FTE: Full time equivalents, *52*
Glossary, *179-186*
Grants, *105-106*
Groups
    agent, *128*
Half-hour segment index factor, *44*
Headsets, *145, 147*
Health & Safety, *121-122, 144-147*
Hybrid ACDs, *71, 75*
Hypertext link, *96-97*
Idle, *36*
Image processing, *96*
Incentives, *105-106*
Index factor, *43-44, 52-53*
Insurances, *141-142*

Interactive voice response: IVR, *79, 90-
91, 141, 152*
Interflow, *125-126*
Internet, *96-98*
Interview, *15-18*
    over the telephone, *15-16*
Intraflow, *66, 111*
Job descriptions, *10-11*
Legislation, *14, 103-104, 120, 133,145-
146,160*
Lighting, *118-119, 146*
Line utilisation, *54*
Management
    information Services:MIS, *57-68, 74,
    79, 107-108, 130*
    performance, *25-34*
    project, *101-133*
    workforce, *94*
Messaging & Music on Hold, *36, 70, 72-
73, 74, 79, 126-127*
Monitoring, *73, 104*
Monthly trend, *39, 43*
Multi-media, *95-98*
Multi-skilling, *21, 100*
Neck and back strain, *145, 146*
Night service, *74*
NORTEL, *71, 167-177*
Occupancy, *36, 49-51, 59*
Operations, *134-166*
Outsourcing, *111-115, 141*
Overflow, *125-126*
Pacific Bell experiment, *154-157*
PBX:Private automated branch
    exchange, *71*
PC based ACDs, *71-75*
Performance
    management, *25-34*
    related Pay:PRP, *26-28*
Pooling principal, *21, 50*
Power, *119*
    fails, *142*
Power dialling, *81-84*
    manual dialling, *81*
    predictive dialling, 79, *82*
    preview dialling, *81, 89*
    progressive dialling, *82*
    screen dialling, *81*

Project Management, *101-133*
Protocols, *85*
Psychometric testing, *17-18*
Queues, *125*
Queue Time, *36*
Random variation, *39, 43*
Ready, *36, 129*
Recorded announcements, *36, 72-73,*
74, 79, 126-127
Recording, *73, 104*
Recovery options, *139-143*
Recruitment, *10-18, 102-104*
agencies, *13-14*
Remuneration, *26-28, 103*
Repetitive strain injury, *144-147*
Reports
agent, *57, 58-61*
call, *57, 61*
daily, *57*
historical, *57, 66-67*
interval, *57*
MIS, *57-68, 74, 79, 107-108, 130*
real time, *65, 67*
trunk, *54, 57*
Ring Time, *36*
Risk assessment, *135-138*
Rostered staff factor, *52*
Screen
dialling, *81*
glare, *118, 146*
popping, *79, 88-89*
Scripting, *99-100*
Seasonality variation, *39, 40, 43*
Seating, *145-146*
Service
agency, *111-115*
levels, *35-68, 114, 130*
Short Calls, *60*
Shrinkage, *51-52, 152*
Siting, *102-106*
Skill development, *19-24*
Soft ACD, *75*
Space, *117, 120, 122*
Speech recognition, *90-91*
Speed of answer, *36, 55*
Staff scheduling, *20, 47-53, 94*
Stand Alone ACD, *75*

Strain,
back, *145*
eye, *146*
neck, *145*
repetitive strain injury, *144-145*
Switch, *36*
Tariffs, *104-105*
Talk time, *36, 59*
TAPI, *86-87*
Telecommuting, *153-160*
Teleworking, *153-160*
Temperature, *121*
Tender
for ACD, *76-78, 107-110*
for outsourcing, *112-114*
Third party CTI, *86-87, 89*
Tie line, *127*
Top and tail recordings, *91-92*
Training, *19-24, 152*
Trends, *39-43*
Trunks, *54-56, 140*
Trunk Hold Time, *36*
TSAPI, *86-87*
Turret, *128-130*
VDU legislation, *146*
Video, *95*
Voice
forms, *93*
mail, *64, 92, 141*
processing, *90-93*
recording, *73, 104*
Wallboards, *25, 74*
Weights, *38*
Workload, *55*
Workforce management, *94*
Workstations, *119-120*
Wrap Up, *36, 59, 73, 128, 130*